Quick Reference Guide™

Word 7 for
Windows® 95

D1072328

Don Gosselin

DDC *Publishing*

14 East 38 St New York, NY 10016

AUTHOR'S STATEMENT

This manual is a quick reference guide for specific tasks in Word for Windows 95 version 7.0. Step-by-step instructions are provided so that either a mouse or keyboard can be used to easily carry out a desired action.

*For exercises and instruction on Word, refer to **DDC's Learning Word for Windows 95 Version 7.0** and **Learning Microsoft Office for Windows 95**. For more information on the Windows 95 operating system, refer to **DDC's Learning Windows 95** and **DDC's Quick Reference Guide** for Windows 95.*

I would like to thank Kathy Suemi Kong, David Gosselin, Dennis Bourgault, Daryl Gray, and my family, for their unwavering support. A very special thanks to my friend and colleague, George T. Lynch. This effort would not have been possible without George's assistance.

Author:	*Don Gosselin*
Managing Editor:	*Kathy Berkemeyer*
English Editors:	*Rebecca Fiala*
	Jennifer Harris
Technical Editor:	*Natalie Young*
Layout:	*Don Gosselin*
	Kathy Berkemeyer

TABLE OF CONTENTS

continued...

ii

continued...

continued...

TABLE OF CONTENTS (CONTINUED)

continued...

TABLE OF CONTENTS (CONTINUED)

continued...

continued...

TABLE OF CONTENTS (CONTINUED)

continued..

viii

continued...

TABLE OF CONTENTS (CONTINUED)

INTRODUCTION

WHAT THIS MANUAL COVERS

The twelve sections in this manual are broken down as follows:

Introduction
Contains information on how to use this manual

Basics
Covers basic information on using Word, including how to move, copy, print, and access Help.

Manage Files
Explains how to work with files. Opening, closing, and saving, for example, are covered here.

Display Options
Covers the various display options available in Word.

Format/Edit
Contains information on the various ways of formatting and editing information in a document.

Tables
Explains how to create and format tables in a Word document.

References
Explains how to reference information such as footnotes, indexes, tables of contents, and bookmarks in a Word document.

Proofing Tools
Explains how to use the various proofing tools in Word, including spell checking, grammar checking, and the thesaurus.

Mail Options
Explains how to create a mail merge, and how to create envelopes and labels.

Compound Documents
Describes how to create and manage compound documents.

Program Options
Describes the different customization and program options available in Word.

COMMAND EXAMPLES

Most commands in Word can be executed using the mouse or the keyboard. Distinct procedures for performing the same task (such as a menu-driven command or by using the mouse) are broken down into separate subheadings. In some cases, however, mouse and keyboard steps are combined, as in the following example:

---

1. Click **File** menu .... **Alt** + **F**

---

*To select this item, mouse users click on File (located on the menu bar), while keyboard users hold down **Alt** and press F.*

*In other cases, mouse and keyboard techniques are separated by **OR**. Generally, mouse steps are given first, followed by the corresponding keyboard step. Available keystroke shortcuts are listed last:*

---

1. Click **File Open** button ....
   in **Standard** toolbar.

   OR

   a. Select **File** menu.. **Alt** + **F**

   b. Select **Open** .... **Alt** + **O**

   OR

   Press **Ctrl+O** .... **Ctrl** + **O**

---

*When you see keyboard characters to the right of a step in reverse type (e.g., **Alt** + **F**), type them exactly as they appear. When you see a substitution word to the right of a step, in place of reverse keyboard characters (e.g., text), replace it with the required value, such as text or a number.*

When selecting information in Word dialog boxes, you can often double-click to select a particular item. Other types of information such as number settings can often be increased or decreased by clicking scroll arrows. Note that these procedures are not always included in the command examples given in this manual.

continued...

xii

COMMAND EXAMPLES (CONTINUED)

In addition to the command examples given in this manual, other techniques for executing a given task probably exist. The techniques listed here represent the easiest and most commonly used procedures.

TOOLBARS

*Toolbars contain buttons allowing you to access many Word commands quickly by clicking with the mouse. Word allows you to display a number of different toolbar sets, as well as allowing you to create your own. (See **TOOLBAR OPTIONS**, page 59, for more information. Also see your Word documentation or on-line **Help** for information on creating your own toolbar sets.)*

SHORTCUT MENUS

*Many Word commands can also be accessed from **Shortcut Menus**. Shortcut menus contain commands related to the item you are working with, and appear in the document window, next to your work area. The available commands in a shortcut menu will vary depending on the selected information.*

EXAMPLE OF A SHORTCUT MENU:

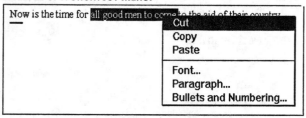

*To access a shortcut menu, select the desired text or item you want to work with, then click the right mouse button or press **Shift+F10**.*

UNITS OF MEASURE

*Since the standard unit of measure used for most Word commands is inches, most measurements given in this manual are also in inches. However, different units of measure can be typed into certain sections of various dialog boxes. Other measurements that can be used in Word are points, picas, centimeters, and lines. (See **GENERAL OPTIONS**, page 266, for information on changing the default unit of measurement.)*

PREVIEWS IN DIALOG BOXES

Many dialog boxes in Word contain **Preview** *boxes displaying a graphic representation of how a particular selection will look in your document. For example, the* **Preview** *box in the* **Font** *dialog box displays an example of the selected font, point size, and other style characteristics.* (See below).

EXAMPLE OF THE PREVIEW BOX IN THE FONTS DIALOG BOX:

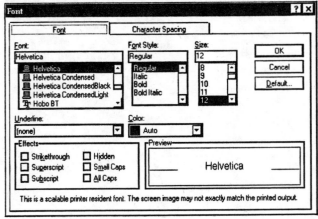

BASICS

PARTS OF THE WORD SCREEN

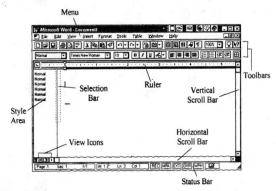

COPY

*Copies selected information to the Clipboard. (See **PASTE**, page 16, for more information.)*

1. Select information you want to copy.

2. Click **Copy** button...
    in **Standard** toolbar.

    OR

    a. Click **Edit** menu.. `Alt`+`E`

    b. Click **Copy**... `C`

    OR

    Press **Ctrl+C**... `Ctrl`+`C`

CUT

*Cuts (or moves) selected information to the ClipBook Viewer. (See **PASTE**, page 16, for more information.)*

1. Select information you want to cut.

2. Click **Cut** button ....
    in **Standard** toolbar.

continued...

CUT (CONTINUED)
> **OR**

> a. Click **E**dit menu .... `Alt`+`E`

> b. Click **Cut** .... `T`
> **OR**

> Press **Ctrl+X** .... `Ctrl`+`X`

DELETE

Deletes selected information from a document.

1. Select information you want to delete.

2. a. Click **E**dit menu .... `Alt`+`E`

> b. Click **Cl**e**a**r .... `A`
> **OR**

> Press **Delete** .... `Del`
> **OR**

> Press **Backspace** .... `Backspace`

DOCUMENT WINDOWS

Arrange All

Positions document windows next to each other as non-overlapping tiles.

1. Click **W**indow menu .... `Alt`+`W`

2. Click **A**rrange All .... `A`

Close Window

(See CLOSE FILE, page 25, for more information.)

Double-click **Close** button .... `✕`
of active document window.

continued...

OR

1. Click **Control** menu .... 🖫
   of active document window.

2. Click **C̲lose**.. C

OR

Press **Ctrl+W**................ .... Ctrl + W

Maximize Window

Fill the Word application window with the active document.

Click **Maximize** box.. 🗗
of active document window
(not available if window is already maximized).

OR

1. Click **Control** menu .... 🖫
   of active document window.

2. Click **Max̲imize** X

OR

Press **Ctrl+F10**... Ctrl + F10

Minimize Window

Reduces active document window to an icon.

Click **Minimize** box .... ▬
of active document window (only visible if window has been
changed to resizeable view with **Restore** command, see
page 6).

OR

1. Click **Control** menu .... 🖫
   of active document window.

2. Click **Mi̲nimize**.. N

Move Window

> NOTE: *A window cannot be moved if it is maximized or minimized. (See **Maximize Window** or **Minimize Window**, page 3.)*

MOUSE

1. Point mouse at title bar of active window and hold left mouse button.
2. Drag window to desired position and release mouse button.

CONTROL MENU

1. a. Click **Control** menu.. 🖾
   of active document window.

   b. Click **Move** .... M

   OR

   Press **Ctrl+F7**.. Ctrl + F7

   The pointer changes to a four-headed arrow.

2. Press an arrow key .... ↑ ↓ ← →
   to move border.

3. Press **ENTER** .... ↵
   when window has reached desired position.

New Window

Opens a new window of the active document.

> NOTE: *Any editing or formatting performed in one window of a document is reflected in all other windows of that document.*

1. Click **Window** menu.................................. Alt + W

2. Click **New Window**.. N

Next Window

> *NOTE:* You can also switch to a different
> document window by selecting the desired
> window from the **Window** menu.

Press **Ctrl+F6** .... `Ctrl`+`F6`

Remove Split

(See Split Window, page 7, for more information.)

Double-click split box ....
at top of vertical scroll bar in bottom pane.

OR

1. Click **Window** menu .... `Alt`+`W`

2. Click **Remove Split** .... `P`

Resize Window

> *NOTE:* A window cannot be resized if it is
> maximized or minimized. (See **Maximize**
> **Window** or **Minimize Window**, page 3.)

MOUSE

1. Point mouse to side or corner of active document
   window until it changes to a two-headed arrow, and hold
   left mouse button.

2. Drag mouse until window reaches desired size.

3. Release mouse button.

continued...

RESIZE WINDOW (CONTINUED)

CONTROL MENU

1. a. Click **Control** menu .... 🔲
       of active document window.

    b. Click **S**ize .... Ⓢ

    OR

    Press **Ctrl+F8** .... Ctrl + F8

The pointer changes to a four-headed arrow.

2. Press an arrow key .... ↑ ↓ ← →
    to move cursor to window border
    you want to resize.

3. Press an arrow key .... ↑ ↓ ← →
    to resize border.

4. Press **ENTER** .... ↵
    when window has reached desired size.

Restore Window

*Adjusts a maximized document window so that it can be moved and resized. (See **Move Window**, page 4, and **Resize Window**, page 5.)*

Click **R**estore box .... 🔲
of active, maximized document window.

OR

1. Click **Control** menu .... 🔲
    of active, maximized document window.

2. Click **R**estore .... Ⓡ

OR

Press **Ctrl+F5** .... Ctrl + F5

Split Window

*(See **Remove Split**, page 5, for more information.)*

Double-click split box...
at top of vertical scroll bar.

OR

1. Click **Window** menu .... Alt + W

2. Click **Split** .... P

The mouse pointer changes to ⬌ and is positioned in the middle of the screen on top of the split.

3. Drag mouse to move split to desired position, and click left mouse button.

    OR

    a. Press **Up** or **Down** arrow key .... ↑ ↓
        to move split to desired position.

    b. Press **ENTER** .... ⏎

DRAG AND DROP

> NOTE: *Drag-and-drop editing can be disabled with the **Edit** tab under **Tools Options**. (See **EDIT OPTIONS**, page 264, for more information.)*

Move

1. Select information you want to move.

2. Point at selected information and hold left mouse button.

3. Drag to new location and position dotted insertion point where you want to move the information.

Mouse changes to drag-and-drop pointer

4. Release mouse button.

Copy

1. Select information you want to copy.

2. Hold **Ctrl** ....

3. Point at selected information and hold left mouse button.

4. Drag to new location and position dotted insertion point where you want to copy the information.

Mouse changes to drag-and-drop pointer

5. Release mouse button.

EXIT WORD

Double-click application **Control** menu ....

OR

1. Click **File** menu... Alt + F

2. Click **Exit**... X

OR

Press **Alt+F4** .... Alt + F4

HELP

The Help menu contains a variety of ways to access help on different Word topics. Also, many dialog boxes include a Help button that opens to help on that particular dialog box. Help comments are also displayed in the status bar when you work with menus or select various commands. Help can also be accessed on different screen elements with the Help button or by pressing Shift+F1.

Word Help is accessed through Windows 95 Help, an extensive program that includes the abilities to view program contents, search for a particular topic, review a history of help topics you have previously looked at, and annotate topics of particular interest. (See your Windows 95 documentation for more information on using Windows Help.)

Microsoft Word Help Topics

*Opens to **Microsoft Word Help Topics**, containing various options for finding help in Word.*

1. Click **Help** menu... `Alt` + `H`

2. Click **Microsoft Word Help Topics**........................... `M`

OR

Press **F1**.. `F1`

Answer Wizard

The Answer Wizard assists you in finding the answers you need quickly using IntelliSense™ technology. This technology helps determine the kind of help you need by allowing you to type in a question using everyday language (e.g., "How do I save my document?").

1. Click **Help** menu... `Alt` + `H`

2. Click **Answer Wizard**.. `W`

*The **Microsoft Word Help Topics** dialog box displays, opened to the **Answer Wizard** tab.*

3. Type a word or phrase describing the task with which you need assistance.

4. Click Search .... `Alt` + `S`

The associated topics display in a list at the bottom of the dialog box.

5. Click desired topic...................................... `↑` `↓`

6. Click Display .... `Alt` + `D`

10

The Microsoft Network

The Microsoft Network is an online service that offers technical assistance and support, as well as Internet access, news, financial information, programs, and many other types of services and features. (See your Windows 95 documentation for information on obtaining an account with The Microsoft Network.)

1. Click **Help** menu .... `Alt`+`H`

2. Click **The Microsoft Network** .... `N`

The Microsoft Network dialog box displays.

3. Click desired topic .... `↑` `↓`
   in **The Microsoft Network** to which
   you want access.

4. Click | Connect | .... `Alt`+`C`

WordPerfect Help

Provides help for WordPerfect users who are converting to Word. This feature allows you to use WordPerfect commands and navigation keys and demonstrates how to accomplish a given task using Word commands.

1. Double-click **WPH** message .... `WPH`
   in status bar.

   OR

   a. Click **Help** menu .... `Alt`+`H`

   b. Click **WordPerfect Help** .... `W`

The Help for WordPerfect Users dialog box displays.

For information on a specific WordPerfect command:

   a. Click **Command Keys** list box .... `Alt`+`K`

   b. Click command .... `↑` `↓`

Information on the equivalent Word command displays in the right hand section of the dialog box.

continued...

c. Click [**Help Text**] .... `Alt` + `T`

to display information as you use
a specific WordPerfect command.

OR

Click [**Demo**] .... `Alt` + `D`

to view a demo on the selected
WordPerfect command.

2. Click [**Options...**] .... `Alt` + `O`

to choose WordPerfect navigation keys
and other help options.

3. Choose from the following Help options:

- Help for WordPerfect Users.................... `Alt` + `W`

- Navigation Keys for WordPerfect Users... `Alt` + `N`

- Mouse Simulation .... `Alt` + `M`

- Demo Guidance.................... `Alt` + `G`

NOTE: ***Help for WordPerfect Users*** *and*
Navigation Keys for WordPerfect Users
can also be selected with the ***General*** *tab*
under ***Tools Options.*** *(See* ***GENERAL***
OPTIONS, *page 266, for more*
information.)

When **Help for WordPerfect Users** *is turned on, the* **WPH** *message*
in the status bar is bold.

4. Click **Demo Speed** drop-down list box.......... `Alt` + `S`

5. Click desired speed .... `↑` `↓`

continued...

WORDPERFECT HELP (CONTINUED)

6. Choose desired Help type:

- Help <u>T</u>ext... `Alt`+`T`

- <u>D</u>emo .... `Alt`+`D`

7. Click ⎡ **OK** ⎤ .... `↵`
   to close **Help Options** dialog box.

8. Click ⎡ **Close** ⎤ .... `Esc`
   to close **Help for WordPerfect Users** dialog box.

About Microsoft Word

*Displays the **About Microsoft Word** dialog box, containing the name of the registered user along with the serial number for the current copy of Word. Also displays the **Microsoft System Info** dialog box, containing a variety of information about your computer and the **Windows** environment.*

1. Click <u>H</u>elp menu .... `Alt`+`H`

2. Click <u>A</u>bout Microsoft Word............................... `A`

   *NOTE: The **About Microsoft Word** dialog box displays.*

   To access Microsoft System Info dialog box:

   Click ⎡ <u>S</u>ystem Info... ⎤ .... `Alt`+`S`

   To access technical support:

   Click ⎡ <u>T</u>ech Support... ⎤ .... `Alt`+`T`

3. Click ⎡ **OK** ⎤ .... `↵`
   to close **About Microsoft Word** dialog box.

TipWizard

Displays tips and examples on how to use Word. The TipWizard automatically tracks your actions and displays helpful suggestions on current tasks.

For a demonstration on how to perform a particular task recommended by TipWizard:

Click **Show Me** button ....

NOTE: *The **TipWizard** can be disabled with the **General** tab under **Tools Options**. (See **GENERAL OPTIONS**, page 266, for more information.)*

Help on Commands and Screen Elements

1. Click **Help** button ....
   in **Standard** toolbar.

   OR

   Press **Shift+F1** ....

The mouse pointer changes to a

2. Press keys for a specific command or click area of screen with which you want help.

NAVIGATE

Go To Command

Moves to different pages, sections, or types of information in a document.

1. Double-click status bar.

   OR

   a. Click **Edit** menu.....................................

   b. Click **Go To** ....

   OR

continued...

14

GO TO COMMAND (CONTINUED)

Press **Ctrl+G** .... `Ctrl`+`G`

The Go To dialog box displays.

2. Click **Go to What** list box .... `Alt`+`W`

3. Click item to which you want to move............. `↑` `↓`

4. Click **Enter** text box.................................... `Alt`+`E`

> *NOTE:* *The name of the **Enter** text box changes depending on the option selected in the **Go to What** list box (e.g., **Enter Page Number**, **Enter Section Number**, etc.).*

5. Type number or select name ....*number* or `↑` `↓`

> *NOTES:* *Choices vary depending on selection made in step 3.*

Type + or - before a number to move forward or back that specific number of items, in relation to your current position (e.g., type +5 to move forward five pages).

6. Click **Next** .... `Alt`+`T`
   to move to next occurrence of item selected in step 3.

   OR

   Click **Previous** .... `Alt`+`P`
   to move to the previous occurrence of item selected in step 3.

7. Click **Close** .... `Esc`
   to exit **Go To** dialog box.

Keyboard
To Move
Press

To Move	Press
One character right	→
One character left	←
One word right	Ctrl + →
One word left	Ctrl + ←
One paragraph up	Ctrl + ↑
One paragraph down	Ctrl + ↓
Next frame or object	Alt + ↓
Previous frame or object	Alt + ↑

To Move
Press

To Move	Press
One column right in newspaper-style columns.	Ctrl + ↓
One column left in newspaper-style columns.	Ctrl + ↑
Up one line	↑
Down one line	↓
Beginning of line	Home
End of line	End
Up one page	Ctrl + Alt + Page Up
Down one page	Ctrl + Alt + Page Down
Up one screen	Page Up
Down one screen	Page Down
Top of screen	Ctrl + Page Up
Bottom of screen	Ctrl + Page Down
Beginning of document	Ctrl + Home
End of document	Ctrl + End
Previous revision	Shift + F5
Location of insertion point when document was last closed	Shift + F5

OVERTYPE MODE

> *NOTE:* You can also type over existing text by
> selecting it and typing.

Double-click **OVR** message .... OVR
in status bar.

OR

Press **Insert** .... Ins

> *NOTES:* When overtype mode is turned on, the
> **OVR** message in the status bar is bold.
>
> The **Insert** key can also be used for pasting
> information from the Clipboard. (See **EDIT**
> **OPTIONS**, page 264, for more
> information.)

PASTE

*Inserts information into your document that was placed on the
Clipboard with the **Copy** or **Cut** commands. (See **Copy**, page 1, and
Cut, page 1; also see PASTE SPECIAL, page 250.)*

1. Place desired information in Clipboard with **Copy** or **Cut**
   commands

2. Place cursor in document where you want to paste
   information from Clipoard.

3. Click **Paste** button ....
   in **Standard** toolbar.

   OR

   a. Click **Edit** menu .... Alt + E

   b. Click **Paste** .... P

   OR

   Press **Ctrl+V** .... Ctrl + V

PRINT

Print Command

1. a. Click **File** menu... `Alt` + `F`

    b. Click **Print**... `P`

    OR

    Press **Ctrl+P**.. `Ctrl` + `P`

The Print dialog box displays.

2. Choose from the following **Page Range** options (default is **All**):

    - **All** .... `Alt` + `A`

    - **Current Page**....................................... `Alt` + `E`

    - **Selection** .... `Alt` + `S`
      (available only if information has been selected in the document).

    - **Pages**... `Alt` + `G`
      Enter page number or page range .... *page range*
      separated by commas (e.g., 1, 3, 5-12).

3. Click **Number of copies** scroll box................. `Alt` + `C`

4. Type number of copies .... *number*
    (default is **1**).

5. Click **Print what** drop-down list box.............. `Alt` + `W`

6. Click type of information to print...................... `↑` `↓`

7. Click **Collate** .... `Alt` + `T`
    to sort multiple copies of a document
    in the correct page order.

8. Click **Print** drop-down list box...................... `Alt` + `R`

continued...

18

9. Click desired print order .... ⬆ ⬇

10. Click **Print to file**.................................. Alt + L
    to print the document to a PRN file
    instead of to a printer.

*This option displays the **Print to File** dialog box, prompting you to
select a drive, directory, and file name for the new file.*

11. Click [**Options...**] .... Alt + O
    for additional print options. *(See **PRINT OPTIONS**,
    page 268, for more information.)*

    To select a different printer:

    *NOTE: This changes the default printer for Word
             as well as all other Windows' applications.*

    a.   Click **Name** drop-down list box .... Alt + N

    b.   Click desired printer .... ⬆ ⬇
         from **Printers** list.

    c.   Click [**Set as Default Printer**] .... Alt + D

    d.   Click [**Properties**] .... Alt + P
         to access options for the selected printer
         (choices vary with different printers).

12. Click [**OK**] .... ⏎

Print Button

Prints the entire active document using the current print settings.

Click **Print** button.. 🖨
in **Standard** toolbar.

REDO

Repeats recent actions, such as typing and formatting.

Repeat Command

Repeats the most recent action.

1. Click **Edit** menu ....

2. Click **Repeat** ....

*The name of the **Repeat** command changes to display the most recent action (e.g., **Repeat Bold**, **Repeat Copy**, etc.).*

OR

Press **Ctrl+Y** ....

Redo Button

Repeats the most recent action or allows you to select from a list of recent actions.

Click **Redo** button ....
in **Standard** toolbar to repeat the most recent action.

OR

1. Click drop-down arrow next to **Redo** button.

A list of most recent actions displays.

2. Click actions you want to repeat.

SELECT INFORMATION

(See SELECT IN TABLE, page 155, for more information.)

Select Entire Document

1. Click **Edit** menu ....

2. Click **Select All** ....

20

Mouse

To Select	Do This
Any item or amount	Hold left mouse button, drag over desired of text information.
A word	Double-click word.
A graphic	Click graphic.
A line of text	Click in selection bar to left of line.
Multiple lines of text	Hold left mouse button, drag in selection bar to left of line.
A sentence	Hold **Ctrl**, click anywhere in sentence.
A paragraph	Double-click in selection bar to left of paragraph, or triple-click anywhere in paragraph.
Multiple paragraphs	Hold left mouse button, drag in selection bar to left of paragraphs.
Entire document	Triple-click in selection bar.
A vertical block of text	Hold **Alt** and left mouse button at the same time and drag.

> NOTE: You can also select information by placing cursor at starting point, holding down **Shift**, and clicking at end of desired selection.

F8 Key

Selects information in a document using the **F8** key, which turns on **Extend Mode**.

> NOTES: When **Extend Mode** is turned on, the **EXT** message in the status bar is bold.

You can also turn on **Extend Mode** by double-clicking the **EXT** message in the status bar.

continued...

Action	Press
Extend selection	F8
Reduce selection size	Shift + F8
Select entire document	F8 five times
Select nearest character (case sensitive)	F8 + character
Select paragraph	F8 four times
Select sentence	F8 three times
Select word	F8 twice
Turns off Extend Mode	Esc

Keyboard

To Select	Press
One character to the right	Shift + →
One character to the left	Shift + ←
Beginning of word	Shift + Ctrl + ←
End of word	Shift + Ctrl + →
Beginning of line	Shift + Home
End of line	Shift + End
One line up	Shift + ↑
One line down	Shift + ↓

continued...

F8 KEY (CONTINUED)

To Select	Press
Beginning of paragraph..........................	Shift + Ctrl + ↑
End of paragraph	Shift + Ctrl + ↓
One screen up......................................	Shift + Page Up
One screen down..................................	Shift + Page Down
Beginning of document......................	Shift + Ctrl + Home
End of document	Shift + Ctrl + End
Entire document	Ctrl + A

SPECIFICATIONS

File Management

Feature	Specification
Bitmap cache	default is 1 MB
Cache size..	512K
Color palette size...	256 colors
Length of Recently Used File list (MRU)	9
Maximum characters per line...	768
Maximum custom dictionary size.....................	366,590 bytes
Maximum file size	32 megabytes (MB)
Maximum length of TOC or index entry	unlimited
Maximum number of bookmarks...............................	32,000
Maximum number of characters in a field.......................	255
Maximum number of characters in fill-in fields...............	255
Maximum number of colors in graphics	256
Maximum number of fields in a document..................	32,000
Maximum number of sorting criteria	3
Maximum number of user dictionaries	10
Number of open documents	limited by memory

Formatting

Feature	Specification
Maximum font size	*1,637 points*
Maximum number of styles	*4,093*
Maximum number of table columns	*31*
Number of fonts	*32,000*
Number of tabs set in a paragraph	*50*

Programming

Feature	Specification
Maximum length for a macro name	*80 characters*
Maximum length for a variable name	*80 characters*
Maximum number of arguments that can be passed to a subroutine	*20*
Maximum size of macro	*limited by available memory*
Supports OLE version 2.0	*yes*

SPIKE

*The **Spike** is a tool that is used for moving multiple items at the same time. Different items can be added to the Spike individually then inserted elsewhere as a group.*

Move Information to Spike

1. Select information you want to move to Spike.

2. Press **Ctrl+F3** .... `Ctrl` + `F3`

3. Repeat steps 1 and 2 for additional information you want to move to Spike.

> NOTE: *You can view the contents of the Spike with the **Edit AutoText Command**. (See **AUTOTEXT**, page 62, for more information.)*

Insert Information from Spike

Inserts information that has been moved to the Spike as a group at the location of the cursor.

1. Place cursor where you want to insert information from Spike.

2. Press **Shift+Ctrl+F3** ....

   NOTE: *Selecting this procedure clears the contents of the Spike. You can also insert information without clearing the Spike by using **AutoText**. (See **AUTOTEXT**, page 62, for more information.)*

UNDO

Undo Command

1. Click **E̲dit** menu... Alt + E

2. Click **U̲ndo** .... U

   NOTE: *The name of the **Undo** command changes to display the most recent action (e.g., **Undo Bold**, **Undo Copy**, etc.).*

OR

Press **Ctrl+Z**... Ctrl + Z

OR

Press **Alt+Backspace**............................... Alt + Backspace

Undo Button

Click **Undo** button ....

in **Standard** toolbar to reverse
the most recent action.

OR

1. Click drop-down arrow next to **Undo** button.

A list of most recent actions displays.

2. Click actions you want to reverse.

MANAGE FILES

CLOSE FILE

Double-click document **Control** menu.............................. 🖻
OR

1. Click **File** menu.............................. Alt + F

2. Click **Close**.............................. C
OR

1. Click document **Control** menu.............................. Alt + -

2. Click **Close**.............................. C
OR

Press **Ctrl+W**.............................. Ctrl + W

> NOTE: If the file has not been saved, you will
> receive a prompt asking if you want to
> save your changes. Selecting **Yes** saves
> and closes the file if it already has a file
> name or displays the **Save As** dialog box if
> it does not. (See **SAVE FILE**, page 43, for
> more information.)

CLOSE ALL FILES

1. Hold **Shift**.............................. Shift

2. Click **File** menu.............................. Alt + F

3. Click **Close All**.............................. C
    > NOTE: If a file has not been saved, you will receive
    > a prompt asking if you want to save your
    > changes. Selecting **Yes** saves and closes
    > the file if it already has a file name or
    > displays the **Save As** dialog box if it does
    > not. (See **SAVE FILE**, page 43, for more
    > information.)

FORMS

Forms can be created in Word that can be filled in on-line or printed out, then filled in on paper. Forms contain **form fields** *which are areas in an on-line form where users can make entries. Three types of form fields can be inserted into a form:* **text**, **check box**, *and* **drop-down**. *Form fields can have macros attached to them as well as customized Help text.*

Forms are usually created as templates and protected so a user can only enter information into form fields.

Create Form

Creates an on-line form.

1. Create new template. *(See **NEW FILE**, page 34, for more information.)*

2. Add desired information and formatting to new form.

3. Follow procedures for inserting form fields under **Form Fields**, below.

4. Click **Protect Form** button.............................. 🔒
   on **Forms** toolbar. *(See **PROTECT DOCUMENT**, page 196, for more information on protecting forms.)*

5. Save and close new template. *(See **SAVE FILE**, page 43; and **CLOSE FILE**, page 25, for more information.)*

Form Fields

Inserts form fields into an on-line form.

TEXT

Inserts a text form field.

1. Follow procedures for creating new forms under **Create Form**, above.

2. Place cursor in document where you want to insert text form field.

3. a. Click **Text Form Field** button........................... |ab|
      in **Forms** toolbar.

continued...

b. Double-click text form field.

OR

a. Click **Insert** menu .... `Alt`+`I`

b. Click For**m** Field .... `M`

The Form Field dialog box displays.

c. Click **Text**... `Alt`+`T`

d. Click ⌜ **Options...** ⌟ .... `Alt`+`O`

The Text Form Field Options dialog box displays.

4. Click **Ty**p**e** drop-down list box...................... `Alt`+`P`

5. Click desired text form type............................. `↑` `↓`

6. Click **D**e**fault Text** text box .... `Alt`+`E`

   NOTE: *Default Text text box changes to*
   Expression text box if Calculation was
   selected in step 5. Option is unavailable if
   Current Date or Current Time was
   selected in step 4.

7. Type text or calculation .... *text*

8. Click **M**a**ximum Length** scroll box .... `Alt`+`M`

9. Type or select maximum length ..... *number* or `↑` `↓`

10. Click **Text** **F**ormat drop-down list box........... `Alt`+`F`

11. Click desired text format .... `↑` `↓`

continued..

FORM FIELDS (CONTINUED)

12. Choose from the following **Run Macro** On options:

- **Entry** .... [Alt] + [Y]

  Click macro .... [↑] [↓]

- **Exit** .... [Alt] + [X]

  Click macro .... [↑] [↓]

NOTE: **Run Macro On** *options runs a selected macro when the insertion point enters or leaves the form field.*

13. Choose from the following **Field** settings options:

- **Bookmark** .... [Alt] + [B]

  Type bookmark name ....*text*

- **Fill-in Enabled** .... [Alt] + [E]

NOTE: *Deselect above check box to make form field read-only.*

14. Click [**OK**] .... [↵]

CHECK BOX

Inserts a check box form field.

1. Follow procedures for creating new forms under **Create Form**, above.

2. Place cursor in document where you want to insert check box form field.

3. a. Click **Check Box Form Field** button .... [⊠]
   in **Forms** toolbar.

   b. Double-click check box form field.

   OR

continued...

a. Click **I**nsert menu .... `Alt`+`I`

b. Click **For**m** Field** .... `M`

The Form Field dialog box displays.

c. Click **C**heck Box .... `Alt`+`C`

d. Click [**O**ptions...] .... `Alt`+`O`

The Check Box Field Options dialog box displays.

4. Choose desired **Check Box Size**:

   • **A**uto .... `Alt`+`A`

   • **E**xactly .... `Alt`+`E`

   Type number .... *number*
   for point size.

5. Choose desired **Default Value**:

   • Not Chec**k**ed .... `Alt`+`K`

   • **C**hecked .... `Alt`+`C`

6. Choose from the following **Run Macro On** options:

   • **Entr**y .... `Alt`+`Y`

   Click macro .... `↑` `↓`

   • E**x**it .... `Alt`+`X`

   Click macro .... `↑` `↓`

   NOTE: **Run Macro On** *options runs a selected macro when the insertion point enters or leaves the form field.*

continued...

CHECK BOX (CONTINUED)

7. Choose from the following **Field** settings options:

- **Bookmark** .... Alt + B

  Type bookmark name .... *text*

- **Check Box Enabled** .... Alt + E

  NOTE: *Deselect above check box to make form field read-only.*

8. Click [OK] .... ↵

DROP-DOWN

Inserts a drop-down form field.

1. Follow procedures for creating new forms under **Create Form**, page 26.

2. Place cursor in document where you want to insert drop-down form field.

3. a. Click **Drop-Down Form Field** button ....
   in **Forms** toolbar.

   b. Double-click drop-down form field.

   OR

   a. Click **Insert** menu .... Alt + I

   b. Click **Form Field** .... M

   The Form Field dialog box displays.

   c. Click **Drop-Down** .... Alt + D

   d. Click [**Options...**] .... Alt + O

   The Drop-Down Form Field Options dialog box displays.

4. Click **Drop-Down Item** text box .... Alt + D

5. Type item .... *text*
   to include in drop-down list.

continued...

6. Click ▢ **Add ▸▸** .... `Alt`+`A`

7. Repeat steps 4 through 6 to include additional items in drop-down list.

   To remove an item from the drop-down list:

   a. Click <u>I</u>tems in Drop-Down List list box.... `Alt`+`I`

   b. Click item you want to remove................. `↑` `↓`

   c. Click ▢ **<u>R</u>emove** .... `Alt`+`R`

   To reorder items drop-down list:

   a. Click <u>I</u>tems in Drop-Down List list box.... `Alt`+`I`

   b. Click item you want to move................. `↑` `↓`

   c. Click **Up Arrow** or .... `↑` or `↓`
      Down Arrow buttons

8. Choose from the following **Run Macro On** options:

   • **Entr<u>y</u>** .... `Alt`+`Y`

     Click macro.. `↑` `↓`

   • **E<u>x</u>it**... `Alt`+`X`

     Click macro.. `↑` `↓`

   NOTE: *Run Macro On options runs a selected macro when the insertion point enters or leaves the form field.*

9. Choose from the following **Field** settings options:

   • **<u>B</u>ookmark**................................. `Alt`+`B`

     Type bookmark name .... *text*

   • **Drop Down <u>E</u>nabled**................. `Alt`+`E`

   NOTE: *Deselect above check box to make form field read-only.*

10. Click ▢ **OK** .... `↵`

Form Field Help

Creates custom help messages to assist users with form fields. (Also see HELP, page 8.)

Status Bar

Adds Help text to a selected form field that is displayed in the status bar while the cursor is in the form field.

1. Double-click an existing form field or Click **Options** button when creating a new form field *(see above)*.

The Options dialog box for the selected form field displays.

2. Click **Add Help Text...** .... `Alt`+`T`

The Form Field Help Text dialog box displays.

3. Click **Status Bar** tab .... `Alt`+`S`

4. Choose from the following **Status Bar** options:

   - **None** .... `Alt`+`N`

   - **AutoText Entry** .... `Alt`+`A`

     Click **AutoText** entry .... `↑``↓`
     you want to appear as Help text in status bar.

   - **Type Your Own** .... `Alt`+`T`
     Type Help text ....*text*
     you want to appear in status bar.

5. Click **OK** .... `↵`

Help Key (F1)

Adds Help text to a selected form field that displays in a message box when F1 is pressed while the cursor is in the form field.

1. Double-click an existing form field or Click **Options** button when creating a new form field (see above).

   NOTE: The Options dialog box for the selected form field displays.

2. Click **Add Help Text...** .... `Alt`+`T`

The Form Field Help Text dialog box displays.

continued...

3. Click **Help Key (F1)** tab .... `Alt` + `K`

4. Choose from the following **Help Key (F1)** options:

   - **None** .... `Alt` + `N`

   - **AutoText Entry** .... `Alt` + `A`

     Click **AutoText** entry .... `↑` `↓`
     you want to appear as Help text in
     message box.

   - **Type Your Own** .... `Alt` + `T`
     Type Help text .... *text*
     you want to appear in message box.

5. Click [**OK**] .... `↵`

Fill-in Form

Fills in an on-line form.

1. Open desired form with **File New** command. *(See NEW FILE, page 34, for more information.)*

2. Click desired form field or use following keystroke methods:

   - Move to next field .... `Tab` or `↓`

   - Move to previous field .... `Shift` + `Tab` or `↑`

   - Display items .... `F4` or `Alt` + `↓`
     in drop-down form field

   - Move to item in open drop-down list .... `↑` `↓`

   - Click or clear check box .... `Space` or `X`

   - Insert tab character into text form field .. `Ctrl` + `Tab`

3. Print, save, or close new form document.

NEW FILE

> *NOTE:* *New templates can also be created from existing documents and templates. (See* ***TEMPLATES***, *page 45, for more information.)*

New File Based on Default Template

Click **New** button.. ⬜
in **Standard** toolbar.

OR

Press **Ctrl+N** .... Ctrl + N

A new document is automatically created based on the default template.

File New Command

Displays the ***New*** *dialog box, allowing you to create a new document or template from any existing templates or Wizards.*

1. Click **File** menu... Alt + F

2. Click **New**.. N

   NOTE: *The* ***New*** *dialog box displays.*

3. Click tab containing template or wizard you want to use to create a new document.

4. Choose desired preview option for templates:

   • Large Icons..

   • List..

   • Details..

5. Click template or wizard................... ↑ ↓ ← →
   upon which you want to base the new file.

continued...

6. Choose file type in **New** option box:

    *   Document.. [Alt]+[D]

    *   Template .... [Alt]+[T]

7. Click [OK] .... [↵]
    to create new file.

OPEN FILE

*The **File Open** command is used for opening and searching for Word documents and files from other applications.*

File Open

Opens existing Word documents and templates, and imports files from various other applications.

> NOTE: *In addition to the **File Open** command, you can also select a file from the recently used file list that appears at the bottom of the File menu. You can use the **General** tab under **Tools Options** to vary the number of recently used files that appear in the list. (See **GENERAL OPTIONS**, page 266, for more information.)*

1. Click **File Open** button ....
    in **Standard** toolbar.

    OR

    a. Click **File** menu................................ [Alt]+[F]

    b. Click **Open** .... [O]

    OR

    Press **Ctrl+O** .... [Ctrl]+[O]

*The **Open** dialog box displays.*

continued...

FILE OPEN (CONTINUED)

2. Click desired dialog box display option:

- List... 🔲

- Details .... 🔳

- Properties .... 🔳

- Preview .... 🔳

3. Click **Look in** drop-down list box .... [Alt]+[I]

4. Click drive containing file you want to open ..... [↑][↓]

5. Double-click folder and subfolders containing file in the list beneath **Look in** drop-down list box.

    To change to previous folder level:

    Click **Up One Level** button.. 🔲

    To open Favorites folder:

    Click **Favorites** button .... 🔲

    To add current folder to Favorites folder:

    Click **Add to Favorites** button .... 🔲

6. Click file name you want to open .... [↑][↓]
    in list beneath **Look in** drop-down list box.

    *NOTE: File names in the list beneath the **Look in**
    drop-down list box are located **beneath** the
    open folders and subfolders.*

    To access additional commands and settings:

    Click **Commands and Settings** icon....................... 🔲

7. Click [OK   ] .... 🔲

File Find

Searches for files matching specific criteria.

1. Click **File Open** button .... 🗁
    in **Standard** toolbar.
    OR

    a. Click **File** menu.............................. `Alt`+`F`

    b. Click **Open** .... `O`
    OR

    Press **Ctrl+O** .... `Ctrl`+`O`

*The **Open** dialog box displays.*

2. Click **File name** drop-down list box .... `Alt`+`N`

3. Type of click file name............................ *text* or `↑` `↓`

4. Click **Files of type** drop-down list box .... `Alt`+`T`

5. Type or click file type .... *text* or `↑` `↓`

6. Click **Text or property** drop-down list box..... `Alt`+`X`

7. Type or click text or property .... *text* or `↑` `↓`
    contained in body of document or selected
    as a file property. Enclose phrases within
    quotation marks. *(See **PROPERTIES**, page 38,
    for more information.)*

8. Click **Last modified** drop-down list box .... `Alt`+`M`

9. Click time period .... `↑` `↓`

10. Click ┌─ **Find Now** ─┐ .... `Alt`+`F`

    To create a new search:

    Click ┌─ **New Search** ─┐ .... `Alt`+`W`

Advanced Find

Searches for files using detailed search criteria.

1. Click **File Open** button .... in **Standard** toolbar.

   OR

   a. Click **File** menu .... `Alt`+`F`

   b. Click **Open**... `O`

   OR

   Press **Ctrl+O** .... `Ctrl`+`O`

The Open dialog box displays.

2. Follow steps 2 through 9 under **FILE FIND**, page 37.

3. Click | Advanced... | .... `Alt`+`A`

The Advanced Find dialog box displays.

4. Click **Property** drop-down list box .... `Alt`+`P`

5. Type or click property .... *text* or `↑` `↓`

6. Click **Condition** drop-down list box.............. `Alt`+`C`

7. Click condition .... `↑` `↓`

8. Click **Value** drop-down list box..................... `Alt`+`U`

9. Type value ....*text*

10. Click **Look in** drop-down list box .... `Alt`+`I`

11. Click where to search for files .... `↑` `↓`

12. Click **Search subfolders** .... `Alt`+`H` if desired.

13. Click | Add to List | .... `Alt`+`A`

continued...

To select additional search criteria:

a. Click **A**nd .... `Alt`+`N`

  OR

  Click **O**r... `Alt`+`R`

b. Repeat steps 4 through 13.

14. Click from following additional search criteria:

  • Match a**l**l word forms .... `Alt`+`L`

  • **M**atch case... `Alt`+`M`

15. Click [**F**ind Now] .... `Alt`+`F`

To create a new search:

  Click [Ne**w** Search] .... `Alt`+`W`

To delete a search:

  Click [**D**elete] .... `Alt`+`D`

To save a search:

  Click [**S**ave Search...] .... `Alt`+`S`

To open a previously saved search:

  Click [**O**pen Search...] .... `Alt`+`O`

PROPERTIES

Displays and changes summary and other types of information about the current document.

General

Displays general file information.

1. Click **F**ile menu... `Alt`+`F`

2. Click **P**roper**t**ies... `I`

*The **Properties** dialog box displays.*

continued...

40

3. Click **General** tab .... ⬅️ ➡️

   *NOTE: Use **Windows Explorer** to change specific file attributes.*

4. Click [**OK**] .... ↵

Summary

Displays and changes summary information about the current document.

1. Click **File** menu .... Alt + F

2. Click **Properties** I

The Properties dialog box displays.

3. Click **Summary** tab .... ⬅️ ➡️

4. Click **Title** text box .... Alt + T

5. Type title .... *title*

6. Click **Subject** text box .... Alt + S

7. Type subject .... *subject*

8. Click **Author** text box .... Alt + A

9. Type author .... *author*

10. Click **Manager** text box .... Alt + M

11. Type author .... *manager*

12. Click **Company** text box .... Alt + O

13. Type company .... *company*

14. Click **Category** text box .... Alt + E

15. Type category .... *category*

continued...

16. Click **Keywords** text box.................................... `Alt` + `K`

17. Type keywords.. *keywords*

18. Click **Comments** text box .... `Alt` + `C`

19. Type comments .... *comments*

20. Click **Save Preview Picture**.............................. `Alt` + `V`
    to save picture of first part of document
    for viewing in **Open** dialog box.
    (See OPEN FILE, page 35, for more information.)

21. Click [**OK**] .... `↵`

Statistics

Displays detailed statistics for active document.

1. Click **File** menu .... `Alt` + `F`

2. Click **Properties** .... `I`

The Properties dialog box displays.

3. Click **Statistics** tab .... `←` `→`

4. Click [**OK**] .... `↵`

Contents

Lists portions of the active document such as embedded objects.

1. Click **File** menu .... `Alt` + `F`

2. Click **Properties** .... `I`

The Properties dialog box displays.

3. Click **Content** tab .... `←` `→`

4. Click [**OK**] .... `↵`

Custom

Creates and displays custom properties for active document.

1. Click **File** menu.................................... `Alt`+`F`

2. Click **Properties**................................... `I`

The Properties dialog box displays.

3. Click **Custom** tab.................................... `←``→`

4. Click **Name** drop-down list box.................... `Alt`+`N`

5. Type or click desired property name.. *name* or `↑``↓`

6. Click **Type** drop-down list box .... `Alt`+`T`

7. Type or click desired property type...... *type* or `↑``↓`

8. Click **Value** text box................................ `Alt`+`V`

9. Type desired value............................*value* or `↑``↓`

10. Click **Link to Content** .... `Alt`+`L`
    if desired.

11. Click [Add] .... `Alt`+`A`

    To modify an existing custom property:

    a. Click property .... `Alt`+`P` then `↑``↓`
       in **Properties** list box.

    b. Make desired modifications.

    c. Click [Modify] .... `Alt`+`M`

    To delete a custom property:

    a. Click property .... `Alt`+`P` then `↑``↓`
       in **Properties** list box.

    b. Click [Delete] .... `Alt`+`D`

SAVE ALL FILES

1. Click **File** menu.. `Alt`+`F`

2. Click **Save All**.. `L`

3. Follow steps 2 through 7 under **Save File**, below, for any new, unnamed files.

SAVE FILE

1. Click **Save** button.. ⊞
   in **Standard** toolbar.

   OR

   a. Click **File** menu... `Alt`+`F`

   b. Click **Save**.. `S`

   OR

   Press **Ctrl+S**.. `Ctrl`+`S`

   NOTE: If the file you are saving already has a file name, the file is saved and you are returned to your document. If you are saving a new, unnamed file, proceed to step 2.

   The Save As dialog box displays.

2. Click desired dialog box display option:

   • List..

   • Details ....

   • Properties...

3. Click **Save in** drop-down list box .... `Alt`+`I`

4. Click drive where you want to save file............. `↑` `↓`

5. Double-click folder and subfolder in the list beneath **Save in** drop-down list box where you want to save file.

continued...

44

SAVE FILE (CONTINUED)

To change to previous folder level:

Click **Up One Level** icon .... [icon]

To open Favorites folder:

Click **Favorites** icon .... [icon]

To create new folder:

Click **Create New Folder** icon .... [icon]

6. Click **File name** list box .... **Alt** + **N**
7. Type new file name .... *name*
8. Click **Save as type** drop-down list box .... **Alt** + **T**
9. Click file type .... **↑** **↓**
   (default is **Word Document (*.doc)**).

   NOTE: *The available file types vary depending on choices made during program installation.*

To access additional save options:

Click [**Options...**] .... **Alt** + **O**

*(See **SAVE OPTIONS**, page 270, for more information.)*

To access additional commands and settings:

Click **Commands and Settings** icon .... [icon]

10. Click [**OK**] .... [↵]

   NOTES: *Depending on choices selected in **Save Options**, the **Properties** dialog box may be displayed. (See **Properties**, page 39, and **SAVE OPTIONS**, page 270, for more information.) If the document you are saving is not a Word file, the **Save Format** dialog box displays. Click the button for the format in which you want to save the document.*

SAVE FILE AS

Saves files with a new name and/or with a different file format.

1. a. Click **File** menu.................................... `Alt` + `F`

    b. Click **Save As**... `A`
    OR

    Press **F12**... `F12`

2. Follow steps 2 through 10 under **Save File,** page 43.

TEMPLATES

All documents in Word are based on templates. Templates contain the default settings for documents such as character and paragraph formatting, as well as page and section setup. They also contain styles, AutoText, toolbars, macros, menu assignments, and shortcut keys. In addition, templates can also contain information such as text and/or graphics that are available to all new documents based on that particular template.

*Word uses a special global template, **NORMAL.DOT.** This template can be used like any other template, although it contains global command information such as toolbars, styles, and macros, available to all documents, regardless of the particular template upon which a document is based. Command information contained in other templates, with the exception of styles, can be made available globally with the File Templates command. (See **File Template Command**, page 46.)*

*Word provides a variety of templates organized into three families: **professional, elegant,** and **contemporary**. (See your Word documentation for a complete listing of available templates.)*

*Word also contains special automated templates called **wizards**. Wizards walk you through the process of creating the following types of documents such as memos, letters, and reports. After creating a document using a wizard, you can save, edit, and format it just like you would any other document. Word also contains a table wizard that automates the process of inserting a table into a document. (See **Table Wizard**, page 149, for more information.)*

*(See **NEW FILE**, page 34, for information on creating new documents with templates and wizards.)*

46

Create New

Creates a new template based on an existing document, template, or wizard.

1. Open file upon which you want to base new template.

   OR

   Follow procedures under **NEW FILE**, page 34, for creating a new template.

2. Add desired information and formatting to be part of the new template.

3. Click **File** menu... `Alt`+`F`

4. Click **Save As**... `A`

5. Follow procedures for saving a template under **SAVE FILE**, page 43.

Modify Existing Template

1. Follow procedures for opening a template file under **OPEN FILE**, page 35.

2. Make desired changes to information and formatting contained in template.

3. Save and close file. *(See SAVE FILE, page 43, and CLOSE FILE, page 25, for more information.)*

File Template Command

The File Template command is used for changing the template attached to the current document. This command is also used for copying, deleting, and renaming styles, AutoText, toolbars, and macros, and for specifying global templates and add-ins.

Add-ins are supplemental programs that add custom commands and features to Word. You can write your own add-ins or obtain them from independent software vendors. (See your Word documentation for more information.)

ATTACH DOCUMENT TEMPLATE

Changes the template attached to the active document.

1. Click **F**ile menu .... `Alt`+`F`

2. Click **T**emplates .... `T`

The Template and Add-ins dialog box displays. The template that is currently attached to the active document is displayed in the Document Template text box.

3. Click **Document Template** text box .... `Alt`+`T`

4. Type name .... *text*
   of template you want to attach to active document.

   OR

   a. Click [**Attach...**] .... `Alt`+`A`

   The Attach Template dialog box displays, opened to the path containing Word's template folders.

   b. Double-click folder and subfolders containing template in the list beneath **Look in** drop-down list box.

   c. Click template name you want to attach ...... `↑` `↓`
      in list beneath **Look in** drop-down list box.

   NOTE: *File names in the list beneath the **Look in** drop-down list box are located **beneath** the open folders and subfolders.*

   d. Click [**OK**] .... `↵`

   To automatically update document styles with styles from attached template:

   Click **Automatically U**pdate .... `Alt`+`U`
   Document Styles check box.

5. Click [**OK**] .... `↵`

48

1. Click **File** menu..................................... `Alt`+`F`

2. Click **Templates**..................................... `T`

The Template and Add-ins dialog box displays. Available templates and add-ins appear in the Global Templates and Add-ins list box. Templates and add-ins that are checked are currently loaded globally.

3. Click **Global Templates and Add-ins**............ `Alt`+`G`
   list box.

4. Click templates and add-ins ...... `↑` `↓` then `Space`
   you want loaded globally.

   To add other templates and add-ins to the Global Templates and Add-ins list box:

   a. Click ⬚ **Add...** ⬚ .... `Alt`+`D`

   The Attach Template dialog box displays, opened to the path containing Word's template folders.

   b. Double-click folder and subfolders containing template in the list beneath **Look in** drop-down list box.

   c. Click template name you want to add .... `↑` `↓`
      in list beneath **Look in** drop-down list box.

   NOTE: *File names in the list beneath the **Look in** drop-down list box are located **beneath** the open folders and subfolders.*

   d. Click ⬚ **OK** ⬚ .... `↵`

   To remove a template or add-in from the Global Templates and Add-ins list box:

   a. Click **Global Templates and Add-ins** ..... `Alt`+`G`
      list box.

continued...

b. Click template or add-in............................ ⟦↑⟧⟦↓⟧
   you want to remove.

c. Click ⟦ **Remove** ⟧ .... ⟦Alt⟧+⟦R⟧

5. Click ⟦ **OK** ⟧ .... ⟦↵⟧

ORGANIZER

*Copies, deletes, and renames styles, AutoText, toolbars, and macros
attached to documents or templates.*

1. Click **File** menu .... ⟦Alt⟧+⟦F⟧

2. Click **Templates** .... ⟦T⟧

   *NOTE: The **Template and Add-ins** dialog box
            displays.*

3. Click ⟦ **Organizer...** ⟧ .... ⟦Alt⟧+⟦O⟧

*The **Organizer** dialog box displays, containing four tabs: **Styles**,
AutoText, **Toolbars**, and **Macros**. The available commands in each of
the tabs are identical.*

*The file list box on the left side of the dialog box defaults to the current
document while the file list box on the right side of the dialog box
defaults to NORMAL.DOT. The names of the file list boxes toggle
between **To** and **In**, depending on which file list box has items
selected.*

4. Choose from the following options:

   • Styles .... ⟦Alt⟧+⟦S⟧

   • AutoText... ⟦Alt⟧+⟦A⟧

   • Toolbars... ⟦Alt⟧+⟦T⟧

   • Macros.. ⟦Alt⟧+⟦M⟧

continued...

ORGANIZER (CONTINUED)

To display a different document or template:

a. Click **Av̲ailable In** drop-down list box ..... `Alt`+`V`
   for file list box on left side of dialog box.
   OR

   Click **Availab̲le In** drop-down list box ..... `Alt`+`B`
   for file list box on right side of dialog box.

b. Click document or template........................ `↑` `↓`

To open different document or template:

a. Click [**Close F̲ile**] .... `Alt`+`F`
   for file list box on left side of dialog box.
   OR

   Click [**Clos̲e File**] .... `Alt`+`E`
   for file list box on right side of dialog box.

b. Click [**Open F̲ile...**] .... `Alt`+`F`
   for file list box on left side of dialog box.
   OR

   Click [**Op̲en File...**] .... `Alt`+`E`
   for file list box on right side of dialog box.

c. Follow procedures under **OPEN FILE**, page 35.

To copy items between different documents and templates:

a. Click item you want to copy in **In** or **To** list box.

NOTE: *Select multiple items by holding down*
        Shift *with above procedures. Select*
        multiple, non-contiguous items by holding
        *down **Ctrl** and clicking with the mouse.*

b. Click [**C̲opy ▸▸**] .... `Alt`+`C`
   for file list box on left side of dialog box.
   OR

continued...

Click `◄◄ Copy` .... `Alt` + `C`
for file list box on right side of dialog box.

NOTE: *A prompt displays asking you how to handle any items in the destination file that have the same names as items in the source file.*

To delete items from a document or template:

a. Click item you want to delete in **In** or **To** list box.

NOTE: *Select multiple items by holding down **Shift** with above procedures. Select multiple, non-contiguous items by holding down **Ctrl** and clicking with the mouse.*

b. Click `Delete` .... `Alt` + `D`

c. Click `Yes` .... `Alt` + `Y`
to delete single item.

OR

Click `Yes to All` .... `Alt` + `A`
to delete all marked items.

To rename items in a document or template:

a. Click item you want to rename in **In** or **To** list box.

b. Click `Rename...` .... `Alt` + `R`

The Rename dialog box displays.

c. Type new item name... *text*
in **New Name** text box.

d. Click `OK` .... `↵`

5. Click `Close` .... `Esc`
after choosing desired commands.

DISPLAY OPTIONS

*Word provides many different ways to display and work with documents. In addition to the following choices, various other display options can be selected with the **View** tab under **Tools Options**. (See VIEW OPTIONS, page 275, for more information.)*

FULL SCREEN VIEW

Hides all portions of the screen that are not part of the document, such as the menu, toolbars, ruler, and scroll bars.

1. Click **View** menu .... ⟦Alt⟧+⟦V⟧

2. Click **Full Screen** .... ⟦U⟧
   To exit Full Screen:

   Click **Full Screen** button .... ⟦▣ Full⟧
   OR

   Press **Esc** .... ⟦Esc⟧

MASTER DOCUMENT VIEW

*Displays documents in **Master Document View**, used for organizing and maintaining long documents by dividing them into subdocuments. Word automatically assigns a unique file name to subdocuments based on the first characters in the heading that begins a subdocument. You can work with subdocuments just like you would other documents. Subdocuments are enclosed in a box and have a **Subdocument** icon (▤) next to them.*

*Master Document View is a special type of **Outline View**. All commands that are available in **Outline View** are also available in Master Document View. (See OUTLINE VIEW, page 54, for more information.)*

1. Click **View** menu .... ⟦Alt⟧+⟦V⟧

2. Click **Master Document** .... ⟦M⟧

continued...

MASTER DOCUMENT VIEW (CONTINUED)

**To switch to Master Document View
from Outline View:**

Click **Master Document View** button ....
in **Outlining** toolbar.

*The Outlining toolbar displays in Master Document View, along
with the Master Document toolbar. The Master Document toolbar
buttons and their associated commands are as follows:*

 Create Subdocument button. Creates a
subdocument for selected headings.

 Remove Subdocument button. Removes a selected
subdocument from a master document.

 Insert Subdocument button. Inserts an existing
Word document into a master document as a
subdocument.

 Merge Subdocument button. Merges selected
subdocuments into one subdocument.

 Split Subdocument button. Splits a subdocument
into two subdocuments at location of insertion
point.

 Lock Document button. Prevents a subdocument
from being edited. Locked subdocuments are
represented by a padlock symbol (🔒) below the
Subdocument icon.

NONPRINTING CHARACTERS

*Toggles display of nonprinting characters such as paragraph marks,
tabs, and hidden text. (See VIEW OPTIONS, page 275, for information
on selectively displaying specific types of nonprinting characters.)*

Click **Show/Hide** button .... ¶
on **Standard** toolbar.

OR

Press **Shift+Ctrl+ 8**................................. Shift + Ctrl + 8

NORMAL VIEW

Click **Normal View** button.. ▤
in lower left-hand corner of screen.

OR

1. Click **View** menu.. Alt + V

2. Click **Normal**.. N

OR

Press **Ctrl+Alt+N**.. Ctrl + Alt + N

OUTLINE VIEW

Displays documents in **Outline View**, *used with Word's nine* **heading
styles** *to organize your document. (See STYLES, page 123, for more
information.)*

Click **Outline View** button... ▤
in lower left-hand corner of screen.

OR

1. Click **View** menu.. Alt + V

2. Click **Outline**... O

OR

Press **Ctrl+Alt+O**.. Ctrl + Alt + O

In **Outline View**, *paragraphs that do not use heading styles have a
hollow square symbol (□) next to them. These paragraphs are also
referred to as* **body text**. *Paragraphs that use a heading style and are
followed by body text have a hollow plus symbol (✢) next to them.
Paragraphs that use a heading style but are not followed by any body
text have a hollow dash symbol (□) next to them.*

Toolbar

*After switching to **Outline View**, the **Outlining** toolbar displays. The **Outlining** toolbar buttons and their associated commands are as follows:*

Promote *button. Promotes selected paragraphs to the previous heading style.*

Demote *button. Demotes selected paragraphs to the next heading style.*

Demote to Body Text *button. Demotes selected headings to Normal style body text.*

Move Up *button. Moves selected paragraphs above the preceding paragraph.*

Move Down *button. Moves selected paragraphs below the following paragraph.*

Expand *button. Displays all text under selected paragraphs using heading styles.*

Collapse *button. Hides all text beneath selected paragraphs using heading styles.*

Show Heading Level 1 *button. Displays all paragraphs using heading 1 style.*

Show Heading Level 2 *button. Displays all paragraphs using heading styles 1-2.*

Show Heading Level 3 *button. Displays all paragraphs using heading styles 1-3.*

Show Heading Level 4 *button. Displays all paragraphs using heading styles 1-4.*

Show Heading Level 5 *button. Displays all paragraphs using heading styles 1-5.*

Show Heading Level 6 *button. Displays all paragraphs using heading styles 1-6.*

Show Heading Level 7 *button. Displays all paragraphs using heading styles 1-7.*

Show Heading Level 8 *button. Displays all paragraphs using heading styles 1-8.*

Show All Heading Levels *button. Toggles between showing heading styles only or all heading styles with all body text.*

Show First Line Only *button. Displays first line only of body text paragraphs.*

Show Formatting *button. Displays text formatting.*

Show Master Document View *button. Displays **Master Document** **View**. (See MASTER DOCUMENT VIEW, page 52, for more information.)*

Keyboard

*Formats information in **Outline View** using shortcut keys. Highlight the paragraphs or headings you want to format and select any of the following keystrokes:*

Formatting	Press
Promote paragraph......................................	Shift + Alt + ←
Demote paragraph	Shift + Alt + →
Demote to body text....................................	Shift + Ctrl + N
Move up..	Shift + Alt + ↑
Move down..	Shift + Alt + ↓
Expand text under heading........................	Shift + Alt + +
Collapse text under heading.....................	Shift + Alt + -

Formatting	Press
Show all text or headings..........................	Shift + Alt + A
Display all text..	* (keypad)
Display character formatting......................	/ (keypad)
Show first line or all body text..................	Shift + Alt + L
Show all headings with	Shift + Alt + #

specific heading style (type specific heading style number)

PAGE LAYOUT VIEW

*Displays documents in **Page Layout View**, used for showing and working with the actual size, formatting, and layout of information in your document.*

Click **Page Layout View** button .... 🖹
in lower left-hand corner of screen.

OR

1. Click **View** menu .... `Alt`+`V`

2. Click **Page Layout** .... `P`

OR

Press **Ctrl+Alt+P** .... `Ctrl`+`Alt`+`P`

PRINT PREVIEW

Click **Print Preview** button .... 🔍
in **Standard** toolbar.

OR

1. Click **File** menu .... `Alt`+`F`

2. Click **Print Preview** .... `V`

OR

Press **Ctrl+Alt+I** .... `Ctrl`+`Alt`+`I`

continued...

58

After switching to **Print Preview,** *the* **Print Preview** *toolbar displays. The* **Print Preview** *toolbar buttons and their associated commands are as follows:*

Print *button. Sends the entire active document to print. (See* PRINT BUTTON, *page 18, for more information.)*

Magnifier *button. Magnifies a portion of the page. Click this button, then click the mouse button to zoom in and out. Deselect this button to return to editing mode.*

One Page *button. Displays one page at a time.*

Multiple Pages *button. Displays multiple pages at the same time. (See* ZOOM COMMAND, *page 60, for more information.)*

Zoom Control *box. (See* ZOOM CONTROL BOX, *page 61, for more information.)*

View Ruler *button. Toggles display of horizontal and vertical rulers.*

Shrink to Fit *button. Forces small amounts of text that are creating a new page to fit onto the previous page. Be careful when using this feature, since it actually decreases the font size for the affected text.*

Full Screen *button. Hides all portions of the screen that are not part of the document. (See* FULL SCREEN VIEW, *page 52, for more information.)*

Close *button. Exits* **Print Preview.**

Help *button. Used for accessing Help on a particular portion of the screen. (See* HELP ON COMMANDS AND SCREEN ELEMENTS, *page 13, for more information.)*

RULER

Toggles display of horizontal and vertical rulers.

> *NOTE: Vertical rulers only appear in **Page Layout**
> **View** or **Print Preview**.*

1. Click **View** menu .... `Alt`+`V`

2. Click **Ruler** .... `R`

TOOLBAR OPTIONS

Selects toolbars to display and toolbar options.

> *NOTE: See your Word documentation or on-line
> **Help** for information on customizing
> toolbars.*

1. Click **View** menu .... `Alt`+`V`

2. Click **Toolbars** .... `T`

The Toolbars dialog box displays.

3. Click **Toolbars** list box .... `Alt`+`T`

4. Click toolbars to display .... `↑` `↓` then `Space`

> *NOTES: Other toolbars may be available in this list,
> depending on your current activity. For
> example, the **Print Preview** toolbar
> appears in this list when you are in **Print
> Preview**.*
>
> *You can also display toolbars with your
> mouse by pointing at a visible toolbar and
> clicking the right mouse button. Click the
> toolbar you wish to display in the shortcut
> menu that appears. Toolbars that are
> checked are currently visible.*

continued...

TOOLBAR OPTIONS (CONTINUED)

5. Choose from the following toolbar options:

- Color Buttons .... `Alt`+`O`

- Large Buttons .... `Alt`+`L`

- Show ToolTips .... `Alt`+`S`

- With Shortcut Keys .... `Alt`+`K`

6. Click `OK` .... `↵`

ZOOM

Zoom Command

1. Click **View** menu .... `Alt`+`V`

2. Click **Zoom** .... `Z`

The Zoom dialog box displays.

3. Choose one of the following **Zoom To** options:

- 200% .... `Alt`+`2`

- 100% .... `Alt`+`1`

- 75% .... `Alt`+`7`

- Page Width .... `Alt`+`P`

- Whole Page .... `Alt`+`W`

- Many Pages .... `Alt`+`M`

a) Click monitor icon .... `Tab`

b) Hold left mouse button and drag to select number of pages.

continued...

ZOOM COMMAND (CONTINUED)

NOTE: ***Whole Page*** *and* ***Many Pages*** *options are only available if the document is in* ***Page Layout View*** *or* ***Print Preview***.

To select custom magnification setting:

a. Click **Percent** text box.............................. Alt + E

b. Type number .... *number* for magnification setting.

Zoom Control Box

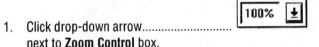

1. Click drop-down arrow........................... next to **Zoom Control** box.

2. Click desired magnification setting.

NOTE: ***Whole Page*** *and* ***Two Pages*** *options are only available in* ***Page Layout View*** *or* ***Print Preview***.

OR

a. Type number .... *number* for custom magnification setting in **Zoom Control** box.

b. Press **ENTER** .... ⏎

FORMAT/EDIT

AUTOTEXT

AutoText entries are stored pieces of information that can be used over again. Examples of AutoText entries are company names, addresses, graphics, and other information that you use frequently.

The names and contents of AutoText entries for the template attached to the current document can be printed. (See PRINT, page 17, for more information.) AutoText entries can also be renamed and copied to other documents and templates using the Organizer. (See ORGANIZER, page 49, for more information.)

Create

1. Select information you want to use to create an **AutoText** entry.

   NOTE: *To store paragraph formatting in the AutoText entry, include the paragraph mark along with the selected information.*

2. Click **E**dit menu.. `Alt`+`E`

3. Click **AutoTe**x**t**... `X`

   The AutoText dialog box displays.

4. Click **N**ame text box.................................... `Alt`+`N`

5. Type name.. *name* for **AutoText** entry (up to 32 characters, including spaces).

6. Click **M**ake AutoText Entry Available To ..... `Alt`+`M` drop-down list box.

7. Click where to make .... `↑` `↓` **AutoText** entry available (default is **All Documents (Normal.dot))**.

8. Click `Add` .... `Alt`+`A`

Insert

EDIT AUTOTEXT COMMAND

Inserts AutoText entries using the Edit AutoText command.

1. Place cursor in document where you want to insert **AutoText** entry.

2. Click **Edit** menu .... `Alt`+`E`

3. Click **AutoText** .... `X`

The AutoText dialog box displays.

4. Choose how **AutoText** entries are inserted into document:

   - **F**ormatted Text .... `Alt`+`F`

   - **P**lain Text .... `Alt`+`P`

5. Double-click **AutoText** entry.

   OR

   a. Click **N**ame list box .... `Alt`+`N`

   b. Type or Click name .... *name* or `↑` `↓` of **AutoText** entry.

   c. Click [**Insert**] .... `Alt`+`I`

TOOLBAR OR KEYBOARD

> *NOTE:* *This procedure automatically inserts AutoText entries as formatted text. To insert AutoText entries as unformatted text, use the Edit AutoText command, above.*

1. Place cursor in document where you want to insert an **AutoText** entry.

2. Type name ....*name* of an existing **AutoText** entry (or the first few letters that uniquely identify an entry).

continued...

64

TOOLBAR OR KEYBOARD (CONTINUED)

3. Press **F3** .... `F3`

   OR

   Press **Ctrl+Alt+V** .... `Ctrl`+`Alt`+`V`

Edit

1. Insert **AutoText** entry you want to edit *(see page 63)*.
2. Make desired changes.
3. Select information comprising **AutoText** entry.
4. Click **Edit** menu... `Alt`+`E`
5. Click **AutoText**... `X`

   The AutoText dialog box displays.

6. Click **Name** text box...................................... `Alt`+`N`
7. Type or Click name .... *name* or `↑` `↓`
   of **AutoText** entry you are editing.
8. Click [**Add**] .... `Alt`+`A`
9. Click [**Yes**] .... `Alt`+`Y`
   when confirmation dialog box appears.

Delete

1. Click **Edit** menu... `Alt`+`E`
2. Click **AutoText**... `X`

   The AutoText dialog box displays.

3. Click **Name** text box...................................... `Alt`+`N`
4. Type or Click name .... *name* or `↑` `↓`
   of **AutoText** entry you want to delete.
5. Click [**Delete**] .... `Alt`+`D`

BORDERS AND SHADING

Thirty different shading patterns as well as a variety of foreground and background colors and border styles can also be applied to paragraphs, tables, and frames.

Format Borders and Shading Command

BORDERS

1. Select desired information to which you want to add border.

2. Click **F**ormat menu... `Alt` + `O`

3. Click **B**orders and Shading .... `B`

The Borders and Shading dialog box displays. The title of the Borders and Shading dialog box changes depending on the selected information (e.g., Paragraph Borders and Shading, Table Borders and Shading, etc.).

4. Click **B**orders tab .... `Alt` + `B`

5. a. Choose one of the following border styles from **Presets**:

   - **N**one .... `Alt` + `N`

   - Bo**x**.. `Alt` + `X`

   - Sh**a**dow .... `Alt` + `A`

   b. Click **C**olor drop-down list box .... `Alt` + `C`

   c. Click border color .... `↑` `↓`

   OR

   a. Click Bo**r**der model............................... `Alt` + `R`

   b. Click side of border model............ `↑` `↓` `←` `→`
      to which you want to add border.

continued..

FORMAT BORDERS AND SHADING COMMAND (CONTINUED)

   c. Click **Color** drop-down list box .... `Alt`+`C`

   d. Click border color .... `↑` `↓`

   e. Click **Style** list .... `Alt`+`Y`

   f. Click border style .... `↑` `↓`

   g. Repeat steps a through f to add borders to additional sides of selected information.

To remove a specific border:

   a. Click **Border** model .... `Alt`+`R`

   b. Click side of border model .... `↑` `↓` `←` `→`
      from which you want
      to remove a border.

   c. Click **None** .... `Alt`+`O`

6. Click **From Text** scroll box .... `Alt`+`F`

7. Type number .... *number*
    for the amount of space between borders and text.

To display the Borders toolbar:

Click `Show Toolbar` .... `Alt`+`T`

NOTE: *This option is not available if the **Borders** toolbar is already displayed.*

8. Click `OK` .... `↵`

SHADING

1. Select information to which you want to add shading.

2. Click **Format** menu .... `Alt`+`O`

continued...

FORMAT BORDERS AND SHADING COMMAND (CONTINUED)

3. Click **Borders and Shading** .... `B`

The Borders and Shading dialog box displays. The title of the Borders and Shading dialog box changes depending on the selected information (e.g., Paragraph Borders and Shading, Table Borders and Shading, etc.).

4. Click **Shading** tab.. `Alt` + `S`

> NOTE: The **Shading** tab is not available if a graphic was selected in step 1.

5. Click **Sha̲ding** list box .... `Alt` + `D`

6. Click shading pattern.................................... `↑` `↓`

7. Click **F̲oreground** drop-down list box........... `Alt` + `F`

8. Click foreground color .... `↑` `↓`
   for selected shading pattern.

9. Click **B̲ackground** drop-down list box .... `Alt` + `A`

10. Click background color .... `↑` `↓`
    for selected shading pattern.

    To remove all custom shading and formatting:

    Click **None**.. `Alt` + `N`

    To display the Borders toolbar:

    Click [**Show T̲oolbar**] .... `Alt` + `T`

    > NOTE: This option is not available if the **Borders** toolbar is already displayed.

11. Click [**OK**] .... `↵`

Toolbar

1. Click **Borders** button .... in **Format** toolbar.

The Borders toolbar displays.

2. Select information for which you want to change borders and/or shading.
3. Click desired icons in **Borders** toolbar.

Automatic Borders

> *NOTE:* *Automatic borders can be disable with the* ***Tools Options*** *command. (See* ***AUTOFORMAT OPTIONS***, *page 256, for more information.)*

To create a thin border line beneath the previous paragraph:

1. Place cursor in an empty paragraph beneath paragraph to which you want to apply a bottom border.
2. Type three dashes ....
3. Press **Enter** ....

To create a double border line beneath the previous paragraph:

1. Place cursor in an empty paragraph beneath paragraph to which you want to apply a bottom border.
2. Type three equal signs ....
3. Press **Enter** ....

BULLETS AND NUMBERING

Bulleted List

Formats selected information as a bulleted list using the ***Format Bullets and Numbering*** *command.*

ADD/REMOVE

Adds and removes bullets from selected information.

1. Select information for which you want to add or remove bullets.

2. Click **Format** menu...................................... **Alt** + **O**

3. Click **Bullets and Numbering**............................. **N**

The Bullets and Numbering dialog box displays.

4. Click **Bulleted** tab.. **Alt** + **B**

5. Click desired format .... **↑** **↓** **←** **→**

   If you do not want the selected information to be formatted with a hanging indent.

   Deselect **Hanging Indent** text box................. **Alt** + **A**

   To remove bullets from selected information:

   Click [**Remove**] .... **Alt** + **R**

   NOTES: This option is unavailable if selected information is not formatted with bullets or numbers.

   *The **Remove** button removes all bullet and numbering options selected from any of the available tabs in the **Bullets and Numbering** dialog box.*

6. Click [**OK**] .... **↵**
   to apply selected bullet format.

MODIFY

1. Click **Format** menu...................................... **Alt** + **O**

2. Click **Bullets and Numbering**............................. **N**

The Bullets and Numbering dialog box displays.

continued..

70

BULLETED LIST (CONTINUED)

3. Click **Bulleted** tab .... `Alt`+`B`

4. Click bullet format.. `↑` `↓`
   you want to modify.

5. Click **Modify...** .... `Alt`+`M`

   The Modify Bulletted List dialog box displays.

6. Click **Bullet Character** list........................... `Alt`+`U`

7. Click bullet character.. `←` `→`

   To select a bullet character not in current list:

   a. Click **Bullet...** .... `Alt`+`B`

   The Symbols dialog box displays.

   b. Click **Symbols From** drop-down list box . `Alt`+`F`

   c. Click font... `↑` `↓`
      containing character you want
      to use as a bullet.

   d. Double-click desired character.

   *NOTE: Dragging your mouse or moving your
            cursor over the character list displays a
            magnified view of individual characters.*

8. Click **Point Size** scroll box .... `Alt`+`P`

9. Type point size... *number*
   for selected bullet.

10. Click **Color** scroll box.................................... `Alt`+`C`

11. Click color... `↑` `↓`

12. Click **Alignment of List Text** .... `Alt`+`G`
    drop-down list box.

continued...

13. Click desired alignment option .... ⬆️ ⬇️

14. Click **Distance from Indent to Text** text box.. Alt + D

15. Type number.. *number*
    for distance from indent to text.

16. Click **Distance from Bullets to Text** .... Alt + T

17. Type number.. *number*
    for distance from bullets to text.

    If you do not want the selected bullet format to include a hanging indent:

    Deselect **Hanging Indent** text box .... Alt + I

18. Click [OK] .... ↵
    to close **Modify Bulleted List** dialog box.

19. Click [OK] .... ↵
    to apply modified bullet format
    to selected information.

    NOTE: *Any information in the current document*
    that is formatted with the modified format
    are automatically updated.

Numbered List

Formats selected information as a numbered list using the Format
Bullets and Numbering *command.*

ADD/REMOVE

1. Select information for which you want to add or remove
   numbers.

2. Click **Format** menu.. Alt + O

3. Click **Bullets and Numbering** .... N

The Bullets and Numbering *dialog box displays.*

continued...

NUMBERED LIST (CONTINUED)

4. Click **Numbered** tab .... `Alt` + `N`

5. Click desired number format........................... `↑` `↓`

    If you do not want the selected information to be formatted with a hanging indent.

    Deselect **Hanging Indent** text box................ `Alt` + `A`

    To remove numbers from the selected information:

    Click [**Remove**] .... `Alt` + `R`

    NOTES: This option is unavailable if selected information is not formatted with bullets or numbers.

    *The **Remove** button removes all bullet and numbering options selected from any of the available tabs in the **Bullets and Numbering** dialog box.*

6. Click [**OK**] .... `↵`
    to apply selected number format.

MODIFY

1. Click **Format** menu .... `Alt` + `O`

2. Click **Bullets and Numbering** .... `N`

    The Bullets and Numbering dialog box displays.

3. Click **Numbered** tab .... `Alt` + `N`

4. Click number format you want to modify .... `↑` `↓`

5. Click [**Modify...**] .... `Alt` + `M`

    The Modify Numbered List dialog box displays.

6. Click **Text Before** text box........................... `Alt` + `B`

continued...

7. Type text .... *text*
   to appear before numbers.

8. Click **N**umber drop-down list box .... `Alt`+`N`

9. Click number style.. `↑` `↓`

10. Click **Text After** text box............................. `Alt`+`A`

11. Type text .... *text*
    to appear after numbers.

    To change font for selected number format:

    a. Click `Font...` .... `Alt`+`F`

    The Font dialog box displays.

    b. Follow the procedures under **CHARACTER FORMAT**,
       page 78.

12. Click **S**tart At scroll box................................. `Alt`+`S`

13. Type starting number... *number*

14. Click **Alignment of List Text** .... `Alt`+`G`
    drop-down list box.

15. Click desired alignment option .... `↑` `↓`

16. Click **D**istance from Indent to Text text box.. `Alt`+`D`

17. Type number... *number*
    for distance from indent to text.

18. Click **Dis**tance from Number to Text .... `Alt`+`T`

19. Type number... *number*
    for distance from number to text.

    If you do not want the selected number format to include a hanging indent:

    Deselect **Hanging Indent** text box................. `Alt`+`I`

continued...

NUMBERED LIST (CONTINUED)

20. Click [**OK**] .... [↵]
    to close **Modify Numbered List** dialog box.

21. Click [**OK**] .... [↵]
    to apply modified number format
    to selected information.

    NOTE: Any information in the current document
    formatted with the modified format is
    automatically updated.

Multilevel List

*Formats selected information as a multilevel list using the **Format***
***Bullets and Numbering** command.*

ADD/REMOVE

1. Select information for which you want to add or remove
    multilevel list formatting.

2. Click **Format** menu .... [Alt]+[O]

3. Click **Bullets and Numbering** .... [N]

    The Bullets and Numbering dialog box displays.

4. Click **Multilevel** tab .... [Alt]+[U]

    NOTE: This option is unavailable if a single
    paragraph formatted with a heading level
    style was selected in step 1.

5. Click desired multilevel format .... [↑][↓]

    To remove multilevel list formatting from selected
    information:

    Click [**Remove**] .... [Alt]+[R]

    NOTES: This option is unavailable if selected
    information is not formatted with bullets or
    numbers.

continued...

MULTILEVEL LIST (CONTINUED)

*The **Remove** button removes all bullet and numbering options selected from any of the available tabs in the **Bullets and Numbering** dialog box.*

6. Click [**OK**] .... ↵
   to apply selected multilevel format.

MODIFY

1. Click **Format** menu.. Alt + O

2. Click **Bullets and Numbering**.................................. N

   The Bullets and Numbering dialog box displays.

3. Click **Multilevel** tab.................................... Alt + U

4. Click multilevel format................................. ↑ ↓
   you want to modify

5. Click [**Modify...**] .... Alt + M

   The Modify Multilevel List dialog box displays.

6. Click **Level** scroll box.............................. Alt + L

7. Click level... ↑ ↓
   you want to change.

8. Click **Bullet or Number** .... Alt + N
   drop-down list box

9. Click bullet or number style............................ ↑ ↓

10. Click **Include from Previous Level** .... Alt + P
    drop-down list box.

    NOTE: This option is unavailable if level 1 was selected in step 8.

continued...

76

MULTILEVEL LIST (CONTINUED)

11. Click number formatting .... ⬆️⬇️
    from previous levels that you want to
    include with subordinate levels.

12. Click **Alignment of List Text** .... Alt + G
    drop-down list box.

13. Click desired alignment option .... ⬆️⬇️

14. Click **Distance from Indent to Text** text box . Alt + D

15. Type number .... *number*
    for distance from indent to text for selected level.

16. Click **Distance from Number to Text** .... Alt + T

17. Type number .... *number*
    for distance from number to text for selected level.

18. Click **Hanging Indent** check box .... Alt + I
    (if desired for selected level).

19. Repeat steps 6 through 18 to change formatting for
    additional levels.

20. Click | OK | .... ↵
    to close **Modify Multilevel List** dialog box.

21. Click | OK | .... ↵
    to apply modified multilevel format
    to selected information.

    *NOTE: Any information in the current document
    formatted with the modified format are
    automatically updated.*

Toolbar

Adds and removes bullets or numbering to selected information using the Formatting toolbar.

1. Click information for which you want to add or remove bullets or numbers.

2. Click **Bullets** button...
   in **Formatting** toolbar.

   OR

   Click **Numbering** button.......................................
   in **Formatting** toolbar.

   NOTE: The most recently used bullet or number format selected with the Format Bullets and Numbering are applied to the selected information.

Automatic Numbered and Bulleted Lists

NOTE: Automatic numbered and bulleted lists can be disable with the Tools Options command. (See AUTOFORMAT OPTIONS, page 256, for more information.)

To create automatic numbered lists:

1. In a blank paragraph, type starting number for list, followed by a period (e.g., "1.") then by a space or tab.

2. Type desired information for first item in list.

3. Press **Enter** ....

4. Repeat steps 2 and 3 for each additional item.

continued…

AUTOMATIC NUMBERED AND BULLETED LISTS (CONTINUED)

To create automatic bulleted lists:

1. In a blank paragraph, type a bullet, asterisk, hyphen, dash, or similar character, followed by a space or tab.
2. Type desired information for first item in list.
3. Press **Enter** .... `⏎`
4. Repeat steps 2 and 3 for each additional item.

CHARACTER FORMAT

Format Font Command

FONT

1. Select text whose formatting you want to change.
2. a. Click **Format** menu .... `Alt`+`O`

   b. Click **Font** .... `F`

   OR

   Press **Ctrl+D** .... `Ctrl`+`D`

The Font dialog box displays.

3. Click **Font** tab.. `Alt`+`N`
4. Click **Font** list box .... `Alt`+`F`
5. Type or Click font............................*font* or `↑` `↓`
6. Click **Font Style** list box .... `Alt`+`O`
7. Type or Click font style .... *font style* or `↑` `↓`

   NOTE: Choices vary with selected font.

8. Click **Size** list box...................................... `Alt`+`S`
9. Type or Click point size .... *point size* or `↑` `↓`

continued...

FORMAT FONT COMMAND (CONTINUED)

10. Click **Underline** drop-down list box .... `Alt`+`U`

11. Click desired underline style .... `↑` `↓`

12. Click **Color** drop-down list box .... `Alt`+`C`

13. Click color .... `↑` `↓`

14. Choose desired **Effects** options:

- Strikethrough .... `Alt`+`K`

- Superscript .... `Alt`+`P`

- Subscript .... `Alt`+`B`

- Hidden .... `Alt`+`I`

- Small Caps .... `Alt`+`M`

- All Caps .... `Alt`+`A`

NOTE: *To set custom superscript and subscript positions, see **Character Spacing**, page 80.*

To use selected options as default settings for the current document and all new documents based on current template:

a. Click `Default...` .... `Alt`+`D`

b. Click `Yes` .... `Alt`+`Y`
when confirmation dialog box appears.

NOTE: *Selecting the **Default** button changes the defaults for options selected in the **Fonts** tab as well as the **Character Spacing** tab (see page 80).*

15. Click `OK` .... `↵`

CHARACTER SPACING

Changes character spacing and kerning for selected text.

1. Select text whose formatting you want to change.

2. a. Click **Format** menu .... `Alt`+`O`

   b. Click **Font** .... `F`

   OR

   Press **Ctrl+D** .... `Ctrl`+`D`

   The Font dialog box displays.

3. Click **Character Spacing** tab .... `Alt`+`R`

4. Click **Spacing** drop-down list box .... `Alt`+`S`

5. Click desired spacing option .... `↑` `↓`

6. Click **By** text box .... `Alt`+`B`

7. Type number .... *number*
   for desired spacing.

8. Click **Position** text box .... `Alt`+`P`

9. Click desired position option .... `↑` `↓`

10. Click **By** text box .... `Alt`+`Y`

11. Type number .... *number*
    for desired spacing.

12. Click **Kerning for Fonts** check box .... `Alt`+`K`

13. Click **Points and Above** text box .... `Alt`+`O`

14. Type number .... *number*
    for point size at which Word automatically
    adjust kerning.

continued...

FORMAT FONT COMMAND (CONTINUED)

To use selected options as default settings for current document and all new documents based on current template:

a. Click [**Default...**] .... [Alt]+[D]

b. Click [**Yes**] .... [Alt]+[Y]
   when confirmation dialog box appears.

NOTE: *Selecting the **Default** button changes the defaults for options selected in the **Character Spacing** tab as well as the **Fonts** tab (see above).*

15. Click [**OK**] .... [↵]

Toolbar

Formatting   **Click**

Fonts............................ [**Times New Roman**] [⬇]

Point Size.. [12] [⬇]

Bold .... [**B**]

Italic .... [*I*]

Underline.. [U]

Keyboard

Formatting

	Press
All capital letters....................................	Shift + Ctrl + A
Bold	Ctrl + B
Create Symbol font	Shift + Ctrl + Q
Display nonprinting characters	Shift + Ctrl + *
Font box (**Formatting** toolbar)	Shift + Ctrl + F
Hidden text	Shift + Ctrl + H
Italicize...	Ctrl + I
Letters - toggle case	Shift + F3
Point size box (**Formatting** toolbar).........	Shift + Ctrl + P
Point size - decrease 1 point...................	Ctrl + [
Point size - decrease to next available point size	Shift + Ctrl + <
Point size - increase 1 point...................	Ctrl +]
Point size - increase to next available point size	Shift + Ctrl + >

Formatting

	Press
Remove formatting	Shift + Ctrl + Z
	OR Ctrl + Space
Small capital letters............................	Shift + Ctrl + K
Subscript...	Ctrl + =
Superscript......................................	Shift + Ctrl + =
Underline - single..............................	Ctrl + U
Underline - double	Shift + Ctrl + D
Underline - word only	Shift + Ctrl + W

Change Case

1. Click **Format** menu.. `Alt`+`O`

2. Click **Change Case**... `E`

The Change Case dialog box displays.

3. Choose one of the following case options:

   - Sentence case .... `Alt`+`S`

   - lower case .... `Alt`+`L`

   - UPPERCASE... `Alt`+`U`

   - Title Case... `Alt`+`T`

   - tOGGLE cASE .... `Alt`+`G`

4. Click [**OK**] .... `⏎`

   *NOTE: You can also toggle the case of selected text by pressing **Shift+F3**.*

Drop Cap

Formats a selected text as a large initial, or dropped, capital letter.

1. Select letter or text you want to format as dropped cap.

2. Click **Format** menu............................ .... `Alt`+`O`

3. Click **Drop Cap** .... `D`

The Drop Cap dialog box displays.

4. Choose one of the following dropped cap position options:

   - None .... `Alt`+`N`

   - Dropped .... `Alt`+`D`

   - In Margin.......... .... `Alt`+`M`

continued...

DROP CAP (CONTINUED)

5. Click **F**ont drop-down list box .... `Alt`+`F`

   NOTE: *This option is unavailable if **None** was*
   selected in previous step.

6. Type or Click font .... *font* or `↑``↓`
   to use for dropped cap.

7. Click **L**ines to Drop scroll box .... `Alt`+`L`

   NOTE: *This option is unavailable if **None** was*
   selected in step 4.

8. Type number of lines .... *number*
   to extend dropped cap downward.

9. Click **Distance from Te**x**t** scroll box .... `Alt`+`X`

10. Type number .... *number*
    for amount of space between dropped cap
    and body of paragraph.

11. Click | **OK** | .... `↵`

Symbols/Special Characters

Symbols and *special characters* refer to symbols and characters that
are not available on the keyboard. They can include bullets, European
letters, trademark symbols, and various other characters.

SYMBOLS

Inserts characters from different character sets.

1. Place cursor in document where you want to insert
   character from different character set.

2. Click **I**nsert menu .... `Alt`+`I`

3. Click **S**ymbol .... `S`

The Symbols dialog box displays.

4. Click **S**ymbols tab .... `Alt`+`S`

continued...

SYMBOLS/SPECIAL CHARACTERS (CONTINUED)

5. Click **Font** drop-down list box .... `Alt`+`F`

6. Click font.. `↑` `↓`
   containing character you want to insert.

7. Double-click desired character.

   OR

   a. Press **Tab** .... `Tab`
      until you reach character list.

   b. Click desired character............................... `↑` `↓`

   c. Press **ENTER** .... `↵`

   NOTE: Dragging your mouse or moving your cursor over the character list displays a magnified view of individual characters.

   To assign selected character to a shortcut key:

   Click [**Shortcut Key...**] .... `Alt`+`K`

   *The **Customize** dialog box displays, opened to the **Keyboard** tab. (See your Word documentation or on-line **Help** for more information.)*

SPECIAL CHARACTERS

1. Place cursor in document where you want to insert special character.

2. Click **Insert** menu.................................. `Alt`+`I`

3. Click **Symbol**... `S`

   *The **Symbols** dialog box displays.*

4. Click **Special Characters** tab .... `Alt`+`S`

5. Click **Character** list box............................ `Alt`+`C`

6. Click desired special character .... `↑` `↓`

continued...

SYMBOLS/SPECIAL CHARACTERS (CONTINUED)

To assign new shortcut key to selected character:

Click [**Shortcut Key...**] .... [Alt] + [K]

The Customize dialog box displays, opened to the Keyboard tab.
(See your Word documentation or on-line Help for more information.)

7.   Click [**Insert**] .... [Alt] + [I]

KEYBOARD

> NOTE: Ordinal numbers (e.g., 1st) and fractions
> (e.g., ½) can be automatically created as
> you type by selecting options with the
> **Tools Options** command. (See
> **AUTOFORMAT OPTIONS**, page 256, for
> more information.)

Special Character   **Press**

Column break .... [Shift] + [Ctrl] + [↵]

Copyright symbol................................... [Alt] + [Ctrl] + [C]

Double closing Smart Quote .... [Ctrl] + [`]

                                    then [Ctrl] + ["]

Double opening Smart Quote............................. [Ctrl] + [`]

                                    then [Ctrl] + ["]

Ellipsis .... [Alt] + [Ctrl] + [.]

Line break....................................... [Shift] + [↵]

Nonbreaking hyphen............................ [Shift] + [Ctrl] + [-]

Nonbreaking space .... [Shift] + [Ctrl] + [Space]

Optional hyphen................................... [Ctrl] + [-]

continued...

SYMBOLS/SPECIAL CHARACTERS (CONTINUED)

Special Character	Press
Page break	Ctrl + ↵
Registered trademark symbol	Ctrl + Alt + R
Single closing Smart Quote.........................	Ctrl + { twice
Single opening Smart Quote	Ctrl + ` twice
Trademark symbol	Ctrl + Alt + T

> NOTE: In addition to inserting **Smart Quotes** with the above keystrokes, you can also set **AutoCorrect** to automatically replace straight quotes with **Smart Quotes**. (See **AUTOCORRECT**, page 190, for more information.)

Copy Character Formats

After applying desired character formats, they can be easily copied to other text in the document.

> NOTE: When using the following procedures, Word copies the character style along with the applied character formatting for the first character in a selection. If a paragraph mark is selected, Word also copies the paragraph style in addition to the character style and applied character formatting for the first character in the selection. (See **STYLES**, page 123, for more information.)

FORMAT PAINTER

1. Select information containing character formatting you want to copy.

continued...

COPY CHARACTER FORMATS (CONTINUED)

2. Click **Format Painter** button ....
   in **Standard** toolbar to copy formatting to a single
   location.

   OR

   Double-click to copy formatting to multiple locations.

The mouse pointer changes to

3. Position mouse over information to which you want to
   copy character formatting.

4. Hold left mouse button.

5. Drag to select information to which you want to copy
   character formatting.

6. Release mouse button.

   If you double-clicked Format Painter button in step 2:

   a. Repeat steps 3 through 6 to copy character
      formatting to additional locations.

   b. Press **Esc** ....
      to turn off **Format Painter**.

KEYBOARD

1. Select information containing character formatting you
   want to copy.

2. Press **Shift+Ctrl+C** ....

3. Select information to which you want to copy character
   formatting.

4. Press **Shift+Ctrl+V** ....

FIELDS

*Fields are used to retrieve and display information in a document
from a variety of different sources. Fields can retrieve information from
other documents, parts of the same document, or from other
applications. Fields can also retrieve information such as the current
time and date from a computer's internal clock and calendar.*

Insert Field Command

1. Place cursor in document where you want to insert a field.

2. Click **Insert** menu.................................. `Alt`+`I`

3. Click **Field**.. `E`
   The Field dialog box displays.

4. Click **Categories** list box .... `Alt`+`C`

5. Click field category.................................. `↑` `↓`

6. Click **Field Name** list box...................... `Alt`+`N`

7. Click field .... `↑` `↓`

   To choose specific options for selected field:

   Click `Options...` .... `Alt`+`O`

   *NOTES: You can also select the **Field Codes** text box and type specific field instructions after the name of the selected field.*

   *This option is not available if **Numbering** was selected in step 5.*

8. Click **Preserve Formatting**...................... `Alt`+`P`
   During Updates check box if desired.

   *NOTE: This option is enabled by default and is not available if **Numbering** was selected in step 5.*

9. Click `OK` .... `↵`

View Field Codes/Results

1. Select fields for which you want to toggle display of codes or results.

2. Point at field and click right mouse button.

The Shortcut menu displays.

3. Click **Toggle Field Codes/Results**.

Keyboard

To Insert	Press
Blank field	Ctrl + F9
DATE *field*	Alt + Shift + D
PAGE *field*	Alt + Shift + P
TIME *field*	Alt + Shift + T

Action	Press
Lock field	Ctrl + F11
Next field	F11
Previous field	Shift + F11
*Run a **GOTOBUTTON*** *or **MACROBUTTON** from field that displays the field results*	Alt + Shift + F9
Toggle all field codes/results	Alt + F9
Toggle selected field code/result	Shift + F9
Unlink field	Shift + Ctrl + F9
Unlock field	Shift + Ctrl + F11
Update linked information *in source document*	Shift + Ctrl + F7
Update selected fields	F9

FIND AND REPLACE

*Allows you to find and replace text, graphics, and other items in a
document. You can also find and replace fonts, styles, and various
other formatting attributes.*

Find

> NOTE: *To quickly repeat the last search, press*
> ***Shift+F4***.

1. Place cursor at position in document where you want to
   begin search.

2. a. Click **Edit** menu.. `Alt`+`E`

   b. Click **Find** .... `F`

   OR

   Press **Ctrl+F**... `Ctrl`+`F`

   *The **Find** dialog box displays.*

3. Click **Find What** text box............................... `Alt`+`N`

4. Type text.. *text*
   for which to search.

   OR

   Select from list of last four entries.................. `↑` `↓`
   you have searched for previously.

   To search for special characters:

   a. Click ┌ **Special ▼** ┐ .... `Alt`+`E`

   b. Choose desired special characters.................... *letter*

5. Click ┌ **Format ▼** ┐ .... `Alt`+`O`

6. Choose formatting for which you want to search.

   To clear all formatting from the Find dialog box:

   Click ┌ **No Formatting** ┐ .... `Alt`+`T`

continued...

FIND (CONTINUED)

> *NOTE:* *You can search for specific formatting without entering any text into the **Find What** text box in step 4. You can also select formatting in the **Find** dialog box by clicking on **Toolbar** options or by using key combinations.*

7. Click **Search** drop-down list box.................. `Alt`+`S`

8. Click direction to search................................ `↑` `↓`

9. Choose additional search options from the following:

    - Match Case .... `Alt`+`C`

    - Find Whole Words Only .... `Alt`+`W`

    - Use Pattern Matching............................. `Alt`+`M`

    - Sounds Like .... `Alt`+`L`

    - Find All Word Forms .... `Alt`+`D`

10. Click **Find Next** .... `Alt`+`F`

    To open Replace dialog box:

    Click **Replace...** .... `Alt`+`R`

*(See the next section, **Replace**, for more information.)*

Replace

1. Place cursor at position in document where you want to begin search.

2. a. Click **Edit** menu .... `Alt`+`E`

    b. Click **Replace**.. `E`
    OR

    Press **Ctrl+H** ....`Ctrl`+`H`

The Replace dialog box displays.

continued...

3. Click **Find What** text box .... `Alt`+`N`

4. Repeat steps 4 through 7 under **FIND**, pages 91 and 92.

5. Click **Replace With** text box .... `Alt`+`P`

6. Repeat steps 4 through 7 under **FIND**, pages 91 and 92.

7. Click one of the following options:

   - | **Find Next** | .... `Alt`+`F`

     to find next occurrence of
     selected information.

   - | **Replace** | .... `Alt`+`R`

     to replace next occurrence of
     selected information.

   - | **Replace All** | .... `Alt`+`A`

     to replace all occurrences of
     selected information.

8. Click | **Cancel** | .... `Esc`
   to close **Replace** dialog box.

FRAMES

In order to view, resize, or reposition a frame, it is necessary to be in Page Layout View or Print Preview.

Insert Frame

> *NOTES: If you are inserting a frame in **Normal View**, a prompt displays asking if you want to switch to **Page Layout View**.*
>
> *You cannot insert a frame from **Outline View** or **Master Document View**.*

FRAME SELECTED INFORMATION

1. Select information around which you want to place frame.

2. Click **Insert Frame** button...................................
in **Forms** or **Drawing** toolbar.

   OR

   a. Click **Insert** menu .... Alt + I

   b. Click **Frame**.. F

INSERT EMPTY FRAME

Creates an empty frame, into which you can later insert information such as text and graphics.

1. Place cursor at position in document where you want to insert empty frame.

   NOTE: Make sure no information is selected.

2. Click **Insert Frame** button...................................
in **Forms** toolbar or **Drawing** toolbar.

   OR

   a. Click **Insert** menu .... Alt + I

   b. Click **Frame**.. F

The mouse pointer changes to a crosshair (+).

3. Position mouse at upper-left corner of where you want frame to appear on page.

4. Hold left mouse button.

5. Drag mouse until frame reaches desired size.

6. Release mouse button.

Format Frame Command

Changes the size and positioning options for a selected frame, using the Format Frame command.

TEXT WRAPPING

1. Click frame.

2. Click **Format** menu.. Alt + O

3. Click **Frame**.. M

The Frame dialog box displays.

4. Choose desired **Text Wrapping** option from the following:

   - None .... Alt + N

   - Around .... Alt + U

5. Click [OK] .... ⏎

SIZE

1. Click frame.

2. Click **Format** menu.. Alt + O

3. Click **Frame**.. M

The Frame dialog box displays.

4. Click **Width** drop-down list box.................... Alt + W
   in **Size** box.

5. Choose width for selected frame:

   - **Auto** .... ↑ ↓
     to adjust frame to width of its contents.

   - **Exactly** .... ↑ ↓

     a. Click **At** scroll box............................... Alt + A

     b. Type number.............................. *number*
        for width of frame.

continued...

FORMAT FRAME COMMAND (CONTINUED)

6. Click **Height** drop-down list box .... `Alt`+`G`
   in **Size** box.

7. Choose height for selected frame:

   - **Auto** .... `↑` `↓`
     to adjust frame to width of its contents.

   - **At Least** .... `↑` `↓`

   - **Exactly** .... `↑` `↓`

   If you selected At Least or Exactly in step 7:

   a. Click **At** scroll box................................... `Alt`+`A`

   b. Type number .... *number*
      for height of frame.

8. Click [**OK**] .... `↵`

HORIZONTAL POSITION

1. Click frame.

2. Click **Format** menu .... `Alt`+`O`

3. Click **Frame** .... `M`

The Frame dialog box displays.

4. Click **Position** drop-down list box................. `Alt`+`S`
   in **Horizontal** box.

5. Click desired horizontal position of frame .... `↑` `↓`

6. Click **Relative To** drop-down list box............ `Alt`+`L`
   in **Horizontal** box.

7. Click where horizontal positioning .... `↑` `↓`
   of frame is measured from
   (in relation to option selected in step 5).

continued...

FORMAT FRAME COMMAND (CONTINUED)

8. Click **Distance from Text** scroll box .... `Alt`+`X`
   in **Horizontal** box.

9. Type number .... *number*
   for distance from text (default is **0.13"**).

10. Click [OK] .... `↵`

VERTICAL POSITION

1. Click frame.

2. Click **Format** menu .... `Alt`+`O`

3. Click **Frame** .... `M`

The Frame dialog box displays.

4. Click **Position** drop-down list box .... `Alt`+`I`
   in **Vertical** box.

5. Click desired vertical position of frame .... `↑`|`↓`

6. Click **Relative To** drop-down list box .... `Alt`+`E`
   in **Vertical** box.

7. Click where vertical positioning of frame .... `↑`|`↓`
   is measured from (in relation to option
   selected in step 5)

8. Click **Distance from Text** scroll box .... `Alt`+`F`
   in **Vertical** box.

9. Type number .... *number*
   for distance from text (default is **0"**).

continued…

FORMAT FRAME COMMAND (CONTINUED)

10. Choose additional desired positioning options:

- **Move with Text**... `Alt`+`M`
  to allow frame to move with paragraph
  to which it's anchored.

- **Lock Anchor**... `Alt`+`K`
  to lock frame to paragraph
  to which it's anchored.

  *NOTE: You can also move a frame anchor to a
  different paragraph using the mouse. (See*
  ***Move Anchor**, page 99, for more
  information.)*

11. Click ▐ **OK** ▌ .... `⏎`

REMOVE FRAME

*Removes a selected frame and inserts its contents above the
paragraph to which the frame was anchored.*

> *NOTE: You can also delete a selected frame,
> although this also deletes any information
> it contains.*

1. Click frame you want to delete.

2. Click **Format** menu .... `Alt`+`O`

3. Click **Frame** .... `M`

The Frame dialog box displays.

4. Click ▐ **Remove Frame** ▌ .... `Alt`+`R`

Mouse

> *REMINDER: To use your mouse to work with a frame, it is necessary to be in **Page Layout View** or **Print Preview**.*

Resize

1. Click frame whose size you want to change.

   > *NOTE: Sizing handles appear on the top, bottom, right, and left edges, as well as in each corner of the selected frame.*

2. Move mouse on top of sizing handle until pointer changes to a double-headed arrow.
3. Hold left mouse button.
4. Drag to desired size.
5. Release mouse button.

Reposition

1. Click frame you want to reposition.
2. Move mouse over frame border until it changes to **Positioning** pointer
3. Hold left mouse button.
4. Drag to desired position.
5. Release mouse button.

MOVE ANCHOR

1. Click frame whose anchor you want to change.

2. Click **Show/Hide** button .... ¶
   on **Standard** toolbar to display nonprinting characters.

3. Move mouse over frame anchor .... ⚓

*Mouse changes to **Positioning** pointer*

4. Hold left mouse button.
5. Drag frame anchor to new position.

continued...

MOVE ANCHOR (CONTINUED)

6. Release mouse button.

> *NOTES: If the frame is not locked, you can display the **Frame** dialog box by double-clicking on the frame anchor.*

*(See **Vertical Position**, page 97, for information on locking a frame anchor.)*

HEADING NUMBERING

Assigns outline numbering to paragraphs that are formatted with heading level styles. (See STYLES, page 123, for more information.)

Add/Remove

1. Click **Format** menu .... `Alt`+`O`

2. Click **Heading Numbering** .... `H`

The Heading Numbering dialog box displays.

3. Click heading numbering format........ `↑` `↓` `←` `→`

    To remove heading numbering:

    Click `Remove` .... `Alt`+`R`

    NOTE: This option is unavailable if heading numbering has not been selected.

4. Click `OK` .... `↵`
    to apply selected heading numbering format.

Modify

1. Click **Format** menu .... `Alt`+`O`

2. Click **Heading Numbering** .... `H`

The Heading Numbering dialog box displays.

3. Click heading numbering format........ `↑` `↓` `←` `→`
    you want to modify.

continued...

MODIFY (CONTINUED)

4. Click | **M**odify... | .... Alt + M

The Modify Heading Numbering dialog box displays.

5. Click **L**evel scroll box................................... Alt + L

6. Click level you want to change .... ↑ ↓

7. Click **Text Before** text box........................... Alt + B

8. Type text .... *text*
   to appear before numbers.

9. Click **Bullet or Number** drop-down list box... Alt + N

10. Click number style... ↑ ↓

11. Click **Text After** text box............................. Alt + A

12. Type text .... *text*
    to appear after numbers.

    To change the font for the selected heading numbering format:

    a. Click | **F**ont... | .... Alt + F

The Font dialog box displays.

    b. Follow the procedures under **CHARACTER FORMAT**, page 78.

13. Click **S**tart At scroll box.............................. Alt + S

14. Type starting number..................................... *number*
    for heading numbering.

15. Click **Include from Previous Level** .... Alt + P
    drop-down list box.

    NOTE: This option is unavailable if level 1 was selected in step 8.

continued...

MODIFY (CONTINUED)

16. Click number formatting .... ⬆️ ⬇️
    from previous levels that you want
    to include with subordinate levels.

17. Click **Alignment of List Text** .... Alt + G
    drop-down list box.

18. Click desired alignment option .... ⬆️ ⬇️

19. Click **D̲istance from Indent to Text** .... Alt + D
    text box.

20. Type number .... *number*
    for distance from indent to text for selected level.

21. Click **Dis̲tance from Number to Text** .... Alt + T

22. Type number .... *number*
    for distance from number to text for selected level.

23. Click **Hanging I̲ndent** check box .... Alt + I
    if desired, for selected level.

24. Repeat steps 5 through 23 to change formatting for
    additional levels.

    To restart heading number at each new section:

    Click **R̲estart Numbering at** .... Alt + R
    Each New Section check box.

25. Click [**OK**] .... ↵
    to close **Modify Heading Numbering** dialog box.

26. Click [**OK**] .... ↵
    to apply modified heading numbering format.

    *NOTE: Any information in the current document
    formatted with the modified heading
    numbering format is automatically
    updated.*

INSERT DATE AND TIME

1. Place cursor in document where you want to insert current date or time.

2. Click **Insert** menu .... `Alt`+`I`

3. Click **Date and Time** .... `T`

The Date and Time dialog box displays.

4. Click date or time format .... `↑` `↓`
   from **Available Formats** list box.

   To insert selected format as a field:

   Click **Update Automatically** .... `Alt`+`U`
   (Insert as Field) check box.

5. Click ` OK ` .... `↵`

MACROS

*A **macro** is a command that you can create to execute a series of pre-defined commands and actions. Macros are an excellent way to automate repetitive tasks. For example, you can create a macro that automatically saves, prints, then closes your document.*

*A macro can be made available to all documents or just documents that are based on a particular **template**. A macro can also be assigned to a **shortcut key** that makes it easier to run.*

Record

1. Click **Tools** menu .... `Alt`+`T`

2. Click **Macro** .... `M`

*The **Macro** dialog box displays.*

3. Click ` Record... ` .... `Alt`+`O`

The **Record Macro** dialog box displays.

4. Type macro name ....*name*
   in **Record Macro Name** text box.

continued...

RECORD (CONTINUED)

5. Click one of the following to run the macro from a toolbar, menu, or the keyboard:

  ● Toolbars .... `Alt`+`T`

  ● Menus .... `Alt`+`M`

  ● Keyboard .... `Alt`+`K`

  NOTE: See **CUSTOMIZE**, page 260, for information on assigning macros and other types of commands to toolbars, menus, and the keyboard.

6. Click **Make Macros Available To**................ `Alt`+`A`
   drop-down list box.

7. Click desired template............................... `↑` `↓`

8. Click **Description** text box........................... `Alt`+`D`

9. Type description for macro.....................................*text*

10. Click [**OK**] .... `↵`

The Record Macro dialog box closes and the Macro toolbar displays.

EXAMPLE OF MACRO TOOLBAR:

11. Perform commands and other actions you would like included in macro.

   To pause while recording:

   Click **Pause** button.. `II●`

12. Click **Stop** button .... `■`
    after selecting desired commands and actions.

Run

Select desired keystroke, menu, or toolbar commands assigned to macro during recording (see pages 103 and 104).

OR

1. Click **Tools** menu .... `Alt`+`T`

2. Click **Macro**.. `M`
The Macro dialog box displays.

3. Click **Macro Name** list box........................... `Alt`+`M`

4. Type or click macro name................................ `↑` `↓`

5. Click [Run] .... `Alt`+`R`

Create/Edit

> *NOTE: These commands open the macro editing window which allows you to edit the **Visual Basic** code of a macro. It is necessary to have a familiarity with programming before attempting to create or edit macros in Visual Basic.*

1. Click **Tools** menu .... `Alt`+`T`

2. Click **Macro**.. `M`
The Macro dialog box displays.

3. Click **Macro Name** list box........................... `Alt`+`M`

4. Type or click macro name................................ `↑` `↓`

5. Click [Edit] .... `Alt`+`E`
if an existing macro name was selected in step 4.

    OR

Click [Create] .... `Alt`+`E`
if a new macro name was typed in step 4.

Delete

1. Click **Tools** menu .... `Alt` + `T`

2. Click **Macro** .... `M`

The Macro dialog box displays.

3. Click **Macro Name** list box........................... `Alt` + `M`

4. Type or click macro name................................ `↑` `↓`

5. Click | Delete | .... `Alt` + `D`

PAGE SETUP AND SECTIONS

*Pages in a document can be divided into **sections**. A section is a portion of your document where you can change layout attributes so they are different from other sections of the document. For example, headers and footers, page numbering, and newspaper-style columns can be different in each section of a document. Until a new section break is inserted, Word treats the entire document as a single section.*

Margins

FILE PAGE SETUP COMMAND

1. Place cursor in document where you want to change margin settings, or select desired information whose margins you want to change.

2. Double-click in blank area of horizontal or vertical ruler.

   OR

   a. Click **File** menu .... `Alt` + `F`

   b. Click **Page Setup**................................... `U`

The Page Setup dialog box displays.

3. Click **Margins** tab....................................... `Alt` + `M`

4. Click **Mirror Margins** check box .... `Alt` + `I`
   to print on both sides of a page.

continued...

5. Choose margin scroll box you want to change:

- **T**op.. `Alt` + `T`

- **B**ottom .... `Alt` + `B`

- **Le**ft .... `Alt` + `F`
  OR

  Inside .... `Alt` + `N`
  (if **Mirror Margins** check box was
  selected in step 4)

- **R**ight .... `Alt` + `G`
  OR

  Outside....................................... `Alt` + `O`
  (if **Mirror Margins** check box was
  selected in step 4)

- **G**utter.. `Alt` + `U`

**Click one of the following to change distance headers
and footers print from edge of page:**

- H**e**ader.. `Alt` + `E`

- Foote**r**.. `Alt` + `R`

*(See **Headers/Footers**, page 115, for more information.)*

6. Type number...................................... *number*
   for distance from margin.

7. Repeats steps 5 and 6 to change additional margins.

8. Click **A**pply **To** drop-down list box .... `Alt` + `A`

continued...

108

MARGINS (CONTINUED)

9. Click where to apply new margin settings........

NOTE: *Choices vary depending on position of cursor in document or information selected in step 1.*

To use selected options as default settings for current document and all new documents based on current template:

a. Click 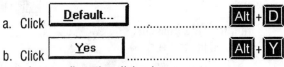 ....

b. Click when confirmation dialog box appears.

NOTE: *Selecting the **Default** button changes the defaults for options selected in the **Margins** tab as well as the other tabs in the **Page Setup** dialog box.*

10. Click  ....

RULERS

*Changes page margins in **Print Preview** or **Page Layout View** using the mouse with the horizontal and vertical rulers.*

1. Switch to **Print Preview** or **Page Layout View**.

2. Place cursor over margin boundaries in vertical ruler for top and bottom margins or horizontal ruler for left and right margins.

Mouse pointer changes to double-headed arrow.

3. Hold left mouse button.

4. Drag selected margin to new position.

5. Release mouse button.

Paper Size

1. Place cursor in document where you want to change paper size and orientation, or select desired pages whose size and orientation you want to change.

2. Double-click in blank area of horizontal or vertical ruler.

   OR

   a. Click **File** menu.. `Alt` + `F`

   b. Click **Page Setup** .... `U`

   The Page Setup dialog box displays.

3. Click **Paper Size** tab... `Alt` + `S`

4. Click **Paper Size** drop-down list box............. `Alt` + `R`

5. Click paper size .... `↑` `↓`

   NOTE: Choices vary with different printers.

   To select custom paper size:

   a. Click **Width** scroll box............................. `Alt` + `W`

   b. Type number .... *number* for paper width.

   c. Click **Height** scroll box........................... `Alt` + `E`

   d. Type number .... *number* for paper height.

   *NOTE: Selecting custom paper width and height changes the **Paper Size** drop-down list box to **Custom**.*

6. Choose one of the following page orientation options:

   • Portrait.. `Alt` + `I`

   • Landscape.. `Alt` + `C`

continued...

110

PAPER SIZE (CONTINUED)

7. Click **Apply To** drop-down list box .... `Alt` + `A`

8. Click where to apply new paper size .... `↑` `↓`
   and orientation.

   NOTE: *Choices vary depending on position of*
   cursor in document or information
   selected in step 1.

   To use selected options as default settings for current
   document and all new documents based on current
   template:

   a. Click `Default...` .... `Alt` + `D`

   b. Click `Yes` .... `Alt` + `Y`
      when confirmation dialog box appears.

   NOTE: *Selecting the **Default** button changes the*
   *defaults for options selected in the **Paper***
   ***Size** tab as well as the other tabs in the*
   ***Page Setup** dialog box.*

9. Click `OK` .... `↵`

Paper Source

1. Place cursor in document where you want to change
   paper source, or select desired pages whose paper
   source you want to change.

2. Double-click in blank area of horizontal or vertical ruler.

   OR

   a. Click **File** menu .... `Alt` + `F`

   b. Click **Page Setup** .... `U`

   The Page Setup dialog box displays.

3. Click **Paper Source** tab .... `Alt` + `P`

continued...

4. Click **First Page** list box .... `Alt`+`F`

5. Click paper source .... `↑` `↓`
   for first page.

6. Click **Other Pages** list box........................... `Alt`+`O`

7. Click paper source .... `↑` `↓`
   for pages other than the first page.

8. Click **Apply To** drop-down list box .... `Alt`+`A`

9. Click where to apply new paper source .... `↑` `↓`

   *NOTE: Choices vary depending on position of
          cursor in document or information
          selected in step 1.*

**To use selected options as default settings for current
document and all new documents based on current
template:**

a. Click [**Default...**] .... `Alt`+`D`

b. Click [**Yes**] .... `Alt`+`Y`
   when confirmation dialog box appears.

   *NOTE: Selecting the **Default** button sets the
          defaults for options selected in the **Paper
          Source** tab as well as the other tabs in the
          Page Setup dialog box.*

10. Click [**OK**] .... `↵`

Layout

1. Place cursor in document where you want to change
   layout, or select desired pages whose layout you want to
   change.

continued...

112

LAYOUT (CONTINUED)

2. Double-click in blank area of horizontal or vertical ruler.

   OR

   a. Click **File** menu .... `Alt`+`F`

   b. Click **Page Setup** .... `U`

   The Page Setup dialog box displays.

3. Click **Layout** tab .... `Alt`+`L`

4. Click **Section Start** drop-down list box .... `Alt`+`R`

5. Click desired section type .... `↑` `↓`

6. Choose one of the following **Headers and Footers** options:

   • Different **O**dd and Even .... `Alt`+`O`

   • Different **F**irst Page .... `Alt`+`F`

7. Click **Vertical Alignment** .... `Alt`+`V`
   drop-down list box.

8. Click desired vertical page alignment .... `↑` `↓`

9. Click **Apply To** drop-down list box .... `Alt`+`A`

10. Click where to apply new layout options .... `↑` `↓`

    NOTE: Choices vary depending on position of cursor in document or information selected in step 1.

    To add line numbers to the selected option:

    Click ⸢ Line **N**umbers... ⸥ .... `Alt`+`N`

continued...

To use selected options as default settings for current document and all new documents based on current template:

a. Click [**Default...**] .... `Alt`+`D`

b. Click [**Yes**] .... `Alt`+`Y`
   when confirmation dialog box appears.

NOTE: *Selecting the **Default** button sets the defaults for options selected in the **Layout** tab as well as the other tabs in the **Page Setup** dialog box.*

11. Click [**OK**] .... `⏎`

Newspaper-Style Columns

FORMAT COLUMNS COMMAND

1. Place cursor in document where you want to change the number of newspaper-style columns, or select desired information for which you want to change the number of newspaper-style columns.

2. Click **Format** menu .... `Alt`+`O`

3. Click **Columns** .... `C`

*The **Columns** dialog box displays.*

4. Choose one of the following column format options from **Presets:**

   • One .... `Alt`+`O`

   • Two .... `Alt`+`W`

   • Three .... `Alt`+`T`

   • Left .... `Alt`+`L`

   • Right .... `Alt`+`R`

   OR

continued...

NEWSPAPER-STYLE COLUMNS (CONTINUED)

a. Click **Number of Columns** scroll box....... `Alt`+`N`

b. Type number.. *number*
of columns.

To change column widths and spacing:

a. Deselect **Equal Column Width** check box `Alt`+`E`

b. Choose one of the following options to change:

- Width .... `Alt`+`I`

- Spacing .... `Alt`+`S`

c. Press **Tab** .... `Tab`
until you reach column number whose width
or spacing you want to change.

*NOTE: The number of columns vary depending on
choices made in step 4*

d. Type number .... *number*

e. Repeat steps b through d to change additional
columns.

5. Click **Line Between** check box...................... `Alt`+`B`
to print vertical line in space between columns.

6. Click **Start New Column** check box............... `Alt`+`U`
to insert column break at position
of insertion point.

7. Click **Apply To** drop-down list box................ `Alt`+`A`

8. Click where to apply column settings............... `↑` `↓`

*NOTE: Choices vary depending on position of
cursor in document or information
selected in step 1.*

9. Click [**OK**] .... `↵`

115

TOOLBAR

> *NOTE: In order to create columns of varying width and other options, it is necessary to use the **Format Columns** command (see 113 and 114).*

1. Place cursor in document where you want to create newspaper-style columns, or select desired information for which you want to create newspaper-style columns.

> *NOTE: Newspaper-style columns are section specific. Section breaks are inserted above and below any selected information.*

2. Click **Columns** button.................................
   in **Standard** toolbar.

A grid displays that is used for selecting the desired number of columns.

3. Hold left mouse button.

4. Drag over sizing grid to select desired number of columns.

5. Release mouse button when desired number of columns is selected.

Headers/Footers

VIEW HEADER AND FOOTER COMMAND

1. Click **View** menu ....

2. Click **Header and Footer** ....

*The header and footer areas displays, enclosed by a nonprinting dashed line, along with the **Header and Footer** toolbar. Information in the body of the document is visible, but dimmed.*

continued...

116

HEADERS/FOOTERS (CONTINUED)

The *Header and Footer* toolbar buttons and their associated commands are as follows:

 Switch Between Header and Footer button. Moves cursor between the header at the top of the page and the footer at the bottom of the page.

 Show Previous button. Displays the previous section's header and footer.

 Show Next button. Displays the next section's header and footer .

 Same as Previous button. Links or unlinks the active header and footer to the previous section.

 Page Numbers button. Inserts a *PAGE* field at the location of the insertion point. (*See* **Insert Page Number Command**, *page 117, for information on selecting different page number formats.*)

 Date button. Inserts a *DATE* field at the location of the insertion point.

 Time button. Inserts a *TIME* field at the location of the insertion point.

 Page Setup button. Displays the *Page Setup* dialog box.

 Show/Hide Document Text button. Toggles the display of information in the body of the document.

 Close button. Closes the header and footer areas and returns you to the body of the document.

(*See* **Layout**, *page 111, for information on creating a different header and footer for just the first page of a section, or different odd and even page headers and footers. Also see* **Margins**, *page 106, for information on changing the distance headers and footers print from the edge of the page.*)

INSERT PAGE NUMBERS COMMAND

1. Click **Insert** menu .... `Alt`+`I`

2. Click **Page Numbers** .... `U`

   The Page Numbers dialog box displays.

3. Click **Position** drop-down list box .... `Alt`+`P`

4. Click desired page number position .... `↑` `↓`

5. Click **Alignment** drop-down list box.............. `Alt`+`A`

6. Click desired page number alignment .... `↑` `↓`

   *NOTE: Selecting **Inside** or **Outside** aligns page numbers close to the inside or outside edge of a page if **Mirror Margins** are selected in **Margins** tab of **Page Setup** dialog box. (See **Margins**, page 106, for more information.)*

7. Deselect **Show Number on First Page** .... `Alt`+`S`
   check box to suppress page numbers
   on first page of current section.

   To change the page numbering format:

   Click | **Format...** | .... `Alt`+`F`

8. Click | **OK** | .... `↵`
   to close **Page Numbers** dialog box.

Insert Breaks

INSERT BREAK COMMAND

1. Position cursor where you want to insert a new break.

2. Click **Insert** menu.. `Alt` + `I`

3. Click **Break** .... `B`

The Break dialog box displays.

4. Choose one of the following break options:

    - **Page** Break... `Alt` + `P`

    - **Column** Break .... `Alt` + `C`

    - **Next** Page... `Alt` + `N`

    - **Continuous** .... `Alt` + `T`

    - **Even** Page .... `Alt` + `E`

    - **Odd** Page .... `Alt` + `O`

5. Click [**OK**] .... `↵`

    *NOTE: You can also insert a column break with the **Format Columns** command. (See **Format Columns Command**, page 113, for more information.)*

Formatting	Press
Column break...............................	Shift + Ctrl + ↵
Line break	Shift + ↵
Page break	Ctrl + ↵

PARAGRAPH FORMAT

Format Paragraph Command

INDENTS AND SPACING

1. Place cursor in paragraph you want to format, or click multiple paragraphs.

2. Click **Format** menu.................................... Alt + O

3. Click **Paragraph** .... P

   The Paragraph dialog box displays.

4. Click **Indents and Spacing** tab .... Alt + I

5. a. Choose one of the following **Indentation** options:

   • Left.. Alt + L

   • Right .... Alt + R

   b. Type number .... *number*
      for desired indent.

   OR

   a. Click **Special** drop-down list box.............. Alt + S

   b. Click desired special indent option.............. ↑ ↓

   c. Click **By** scroll box .... Alt + Y

   d. Type number .... *number*
      for desired indent.

continued...

120

FORMAT PARAGRAPH COMMAND (CONTINUED)

6. a. Choose desired **Spacing** options:

  - Before .... `Alt` + `B`

  - Aft<u>e</u>r .... `Alt` + `E`

  b. Type number .... *number*
  for desired spacing before.

7. Click **Li<u>n</u>e Spacing** drop-down list box .... `Alt` + `N`

8. Click desired line spacing option..................... `↑` `↓`

9. Click **<u>A</u>t** scroll box .... `Alt` + `A`
  if you selected **At Least, Exactly,**
  or **Multiple** in previous step.

10. Type number .... *number*
  for desired line spacing.

11. Click **Alignment** drop-down list box .... `Alt` + `G`

12. Click desired alignment option......................... `↑` `↓`

  To format tabs for the selected paragraphs:

  Click │ **<u>T</u>abs...** │ .... `Alt` + `T`
  (See TABS, page 133, for more information.)

13. Click │ **OK** │ .... `↵`

TEXT FLOW

1. Place cursor in paragraph you want to format, or select
  multiple paragraphs.

2. Click **F<u>o</u>rmat** menu .... `Alt` + `O`

3. Click **Paragraph**.. `P`

The Paragraph dialog box displays.

continued...

FORMAT PARAGRAPH COMMAND (CONTINUED)

4. Click **Text Flow** tab...................................... `Alt`+`F`

5. Choose one of the following **Pagination** options:

   • Widow/Orphan Control........................... `Alt`+`W`

   • Keep Lines Together.............................. `Alt`+`K`

   • Keep with Next .... `Alt`+`X`

   • Page Break Before .... `Alt`+`P`

6. Click **Suppress Line Numbers** .... `Alt`+`S`
   to suppress line numbers for selected
   paragraphs in sections formatted for line numbering.
   *(See **Layout**, page 111, for more information.)*

7. Click **Don't Hyphenate** .... `Alt`+`D`
   to prevent selected paragraphs from being
   hyphenated in documents formatted for automatic
   hyphenation.*(See **HYPHENATION**, page 194, for more
   information.)*

   To format tabs for the selected paragraphs:

   Click [**Tabs...**] .... `Alt`+`T`
   *(See **TABS**, page 133, for more information.)*

8. Click [**OK**] .... `↵`

Toolbar

Formatting	Click
Left align..	
Center align..	
Right align	
Justify...	
Decrease indent...	
Increase indent	

Ruler

1. Select paragraphs whose indents you want to change.
2. Move mouse on top of desired indent marker:
   - First Line Indent.. ▽
   - Left Indent .... ⬠
     (select bottom marker)
   - First Line and Left Indents simultaneously .... ⯆
     (select bottom marker)
   - Right Indent.. △
3. Hold left mouse button.
4. Drag to desired position.
5. Release mouse button.

Keyboard

Formatting	Press
Center align	Ctrl + E
Double spacing	Ctrl + 2
Hanging indent	Ctrl + T
Justify	Ctrl + J
Left align	Ctrl + L
Left indent	Ctrl + M
Open/Remove one line before	Ctrl + 0 (Zero)
One-and-a-half line spacing	Ctrl + 5
Reduce hanging indent	Shift + Ctrl + T
Remove left paragraph indent	Shift + Ctrl + M
Right align	Ctrl + R
Single spacing	Ctrl + 1

STYLES

*Styles can be saved within a template or as part of a document, and can be easily copied between different templates and documents using the **Organizer**. (See ORGANIZER, page 49, for more information.)*

*The names of applied paragraph styles can be displayed at the left side of the document window with the **View** tab under **Tools Options**. (See VIEW OPTIONS, page 275, for more information.)*

Format Style Command

APPLY STYLE

1. Select paragraphs to which you want to apply paragraph style, or select characters to which you want to apply character style.

continued...

FORMAT STYLE COMMAND (CONTINUED)

2. Click **Format** menu .... `Alt` + `O`

3. Click **Style**.. `S`

The Style dialog box displays.

4. Click **List** drop-down list box......... .... `Alt` + `L`

5. Choose one of the following style options you want displayed:

   • Styles in Use .... `↑` `↓`

   • All Styles .... `↑` `↓`

   • User-Defined Styles ... . `↑` `↓`

6. Click **Styles** list box . ... `Alt` + `S`

7. Click desired style... `↑` `↓`

   NOTE: Paragraph style names are bold, character styles are not bold.

8. Click [**Apply**] .... `Alt` + `A`

CREATE STYLE

1. Click **Format** menu .... `Alt` + `O`

2. Click **Style**.. `S`

The Style dialog box displays.

3. Click [**New...**] .... `Alt` + `N`

The New Style dialog box displays.

4. Click **Name** text box.................................. `Alt` + `N`

5 Type new style name ....*text*

continued...

FORMAT STYLE COMMAND (CONTINUED)

6. Click **Style Type** drop-down list box .... `Alt`+`T`

7. Click desired style type option......................... `↑` `↓`

8. Click **Based On** drop-down list box............... `Alt`+`B`

9. Click style... `↑` `↓`
   upon which you want to base the new style.

   NOTE: *By default, new paragraph styles are based on the style applied to the active paragraph.*

10. Click **Style for Following Paragraph**............. `Alt`+`S`
    drop-down list box

    NOTE: *This option is not available if **Character** was selected for **Style Type** in step 7.*

11. Click style.. `↑` `↓`
    to be applied to following paragraphs.

12. Click **Format ▼** .... `Alt`+`O`

13. Choose desired formatting options for the new style.

14. Click **Shortcut Key...** .... `Alt`+`K`
    to assign the new style to a key combination.

    *The **Customize** dialog box displays, opened to the **Keyboard** tab. (See your Word documentation or on-line **Help** for more information.)*

    NOTE: *In addition to shortcut keys, styles can also be assigned to toolbars. See your Word documentation or on-line **Help** for more information.*

15. Click **Add to Template** check box.................. `Alt`+`A`
    if you want to add new style
    to current document template.

continued...

FORMAT STYLE COMMAND (CONTINUED)

16. Click **OK** .... ↵
    to create new style and close **New Style** dialog box.

17. Click **Close** .... Esc
    to close **Style** dialog box.

MODIFY STYLE

1. Click **Format** menu .... Alt + O

2. Click **Style** .... S

   The Style dialog box displays.

3. Click **List** drop-down list box .... Alt + L

4. Choose one of the following style options you want
   displayed:

   • Styles in Use .... ↑ ↓

   • All Styles .... ↑ ↓

   • User-Defined Styles .... ↑ ↓

5. Click **Styles** list box .... Alt + S

6. Click style you want to modify .... ↑ ↓

   *NOTE: Paragraph style names are bold, character
   styles are not bold.*

7. Click **Modify...** .... Alt + M

   The Modify Style dialog box displays.

8. Follow steps 5 through 17 under **Create Style**, page
   124.

DELETE STYLE

> *NOTE: Built-in styles, such as heading level styles, cannot be deleted.*

1. Click **Format** menu.................................... `Alt` + `O`

2. Click **Style**... `S`

The Style dialog box displays.

3. Click **List** drop-down list box .... `Alt` + `L`

4. Choose one of the following style options you want displayed:

   • Styles in Use .... `↑` `↓`

   • All Styles .... `↑` `↓`

   • User-Defined Styles................................... `↑` `↓`

5. Click **Styles** list box.................................. `Alt` + `S`

6. Click style... `↑` `↓`
   you want to delete.

   > *NOTE: Paragraph style names are bold, character styles are not bold.*

7. Click [**Delete**] .... `Alt` + `D`

8. Click [**Yes**] .... `Y`
   when **Delete Confirmation** dialog box appears.

9. Click [**Close**] .... `Esc`
   to close **Style** dialog box.

Toolbar

APPLY STYLE

1. Select paragraphs to which you want to apply paragraph style, or select characters to which you want to apply character style.

2. Click **Style** box.................................. `Shift` + `Ctrl` + `S`
    in **Formatting** toolbar.

3. Click style.

    OR

    a. Click style .... `↑` `↓`

    b. Press **ENTER** .... `↵`

CREATE STYLE

1. Make desired formatting changes to existing style.

2. Click **Style** box.................................. `Shift` + `Ctrl` + `S`
    in **Formatting** toolbar.

3. Type new style name .... *text*

4. Press **ENTER** .... `↵`

CHANGE STYLE

1. Make desired formatting changes to existing style.

2. Click **Style** box.................................. `Shift` + `Ctrl` + `S`
    in **Formatting** toolbar.

3. Press **ENTER** .... `↵`

    The Reapply Style dialog box displays.

4. Click **Redefine the style using** .... `R`
    the select as an example?

5. Click [**OK**] .... `↵`

REAPPLY STYLE

1. Select paragraphs to which you want to reapply paragraph style, or select characters to which you want to reapply character style.

2. Click **Style** box .... `Shift` + `Ctrl` + `S`
   in **Formatting** toolbar.

3. Press **ENTER** .... `↵`

   NOTE: *If the formatting of the selected information has been changed from formatting of applied style, **Reapply Style** dialog box displays. Select **Return the formatting of the selection to the style?** and then select* `  OK  `

Keyboard

Command	**Press**
*Open **Format Style** box in* *Formatting toolbar. Press twice to open Format Style dialog box.*	`Shift` + `Ctrl` + `S`
Remove paragraph formatting *not part of applied style from selected information*	`Ctrl` + `Q`
*Start **AutoFormat***	`Ctrl` + `K`
*Apply **Normal** style*	`Shift` + `Ctrl` + `N`
*Apply **Heading 1** style*	`Ctrl` + `Alt` + `1`
*Apply **Heading 2** style*	`Ctrl` + `Alt` + `2`
*Apply **Heading 3** style*	`Ctrl` + `Alt` + `3`
*Apply **List** style*	`Shift` + `Ctrl` + `L`
Remove character styles from selected characters	`Ctrl` + `Space`

Style Gallery

Copies all styles from a different template to the current document. Displays different previews of the available template styles including a preview of what the document looks like when the new styles have been applied.

> *NOTE:* *Copying styles from the **Style Gallery** automatically overwrites styles in the document with the same style name.*

1. Click **Format** menu .... `Alt`+`O`

2. Click **Style Gallery**.. `G`

The Style Gallery dialog box displays.

3. Click **Template** list box .... `Alt`+`T`

4. Click template .... `↑` `↓`
   containing styles you want to copy.

5. Choose one of the following **Preview** option:

   • Document .... `Alt`+`D`

   • Example .... `Alt`+`E`

   • Style Samples .... `Alt`+`S`

6. Click [**OK**] .... `↵`
   to close **Style Gallery** dialog box and apply styles from selected template.

AutoFormat

(See AUTOFORMAT OPTIONS, page 256, for more information.)

NOTE: *This command does not format tables. To automatically format tables, use the **Table AutoFormat** command. (See **TABLE AUTOFORMAT**, page 160, for more information.)*

FORMAT AUTOFORMAT COMMAND

Allows you to review formatting changes.

1. Place cursor anywhere in document to format entire document, or select desired information you want to format.

2. Click **Format** menu..................................... Alt + O

3. Click **AutoFormat** .... A

A prompt displays, telling you that Word is about to format the document or selected information.

4. Click **OK** .... ↵

   NOTE: *Word automatically formats the document with styles from the attached template, then displays the **AutoFormat** dialog box.*

5. Click **Accept** .... Alt + A
   to accept style changes.

   OR

   Click **Reject All** .... Alt + R
   to reject style changes.

   To review individual style changes:

   a. Click **Review Changes...** .... Alt + C

The Review AutoFormat Changes dialog box displays.

continued...

AUTOFORMAT (CONTINUED)

   b. Choose from the following commands:

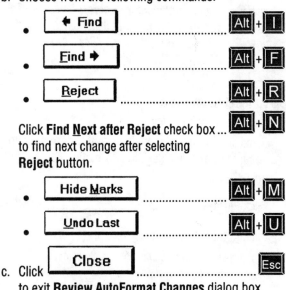

- **← Find** .... **Alt** + **I**

- **Find →** .... **Alt** + **F**

- **Reject** .... **Alt** + **R**

Click **Find Next after Reject** check box ... **Alt** + **N**
to find next change after selecting
Reject button.

- **Hide Marks** .... **Alt** + **M**

- **Undo Last** .... **Alt** + **U**

   c. Click **Close** .... **Esc**
     to exit **Review AutoFormat Changes** dialog box.

The AutoFormat dialog box redisplays.

To choose styles from different template:

Click **Style Gallery...** .... **Alt** + **S**
*(See **Style Gallery**, page 130, for more information.)*

TOOLBAR OR KEYBOARD

*Automatically formats documents or selected information using the
AutoFormat button in the Standard toolbar or by pressing Ctrl+K.
This command does not allow you to review formatting changes, as
does the Format AutoFormat command (see above).*

1. Place cursor anywhere in document to format entire
document, or select information you want to format.

2. Click **AutoFormat** button....................................
in **Standard** toolbar.

   OR

continued...

AUTOFORMAT (CONTINUED)

Press **Ctrl+K**...`Ctrl`+`K`

NOTE: The document or selected information is
        automatically formatted according to the
        options selected in the **AutoFormat** tab
        under **Tools Options**.

Automatic Headings

NOTE: Automatic headings can be disable with the
        Tools Options command. (See
        AUTOFORMAT OPTIONS, page 256, for
        more information.)

To automatically format a paragraph with Heading 1 style:

1. Type desired text...................................... *text*
    for heading.

2. Press **Enter** twice .... `←` `←`

To automatically format a paragraph with Heading 2 style:

1. Press **Tab**.. `Tab`
    OR
    Begin paragraph with a half-inch indent.

2. Type desired text...................................... *text*
    for heading.

TABS

Format Tabs Command

SET/CHANGE TAB STOP

1. Select paragraphs for which you want to format tab
    stops.

2. Double-click existing tab in horizontal ruler.

    OR

continued...

FORMAT TABS COMMAND (CONTINUED)

    a. Click **F**o**rmat** menu .... `Alt` + `O`

    b. Click **T**abs .... `T`

The **Tabs** *dialog box displays.*

3. Click **T**ab **Stop Position** list box .... `Alt` + `T`

4. Type number .... *number*
    for tab stop position.

5. Choose one of the following **Alignment** options:

    • **L**eft .... `Alt` + `L`

    • **C**enter .... `Alt` + `C`

    • **R**ight .... `Alt` + `R`

    • **D**ecimal .... `Alt` + `D`

    • **B**ar .... `Alt` + `B`

6. Choose desired **Leader** option.

7. Click   **S**et   .... `Alt` + `S`

8. Repeat steps 4 through 8 to set additional tab stops.

9. Click   **OK**   .... `↵`

Remove Individual Tab Stop

1. Select paragraphs for which you want to remove tab stops.

2. Click **Format** menu.. `Alt`+`O`

3. Click **T**abs .... `T`

The Tabs dialog box displays.

4. Click **T**ab Stop Position list box .... `Alt`+`T`

5. Click tab stop .... `↑` `↓`
   you want to remove.

6. Click ⬚ **Cl<u>e</u>ar** .... `Alt`+`E`

7. Repeat steps 4 through 6 to remove additional tab stops.

8. Click ⬚ **OK** .... `↵`

Remove All Tab Stops

1. Select paragraphs for which you want to remove tab stops.

2. Click **Format** menu.. `Alt`+`O`

3. Click **T**abs .... `T`

The Tabs dialog box displays.

4. Click ⬚ **Clear <u>A</u>ll** .... `Alt`+`A`

5. Click ⬚ **OK** .... `↵`

Default Tab Stops

   NOTE: Default tab stops cannot be set for individual paragraphs, only for an entire document.

1. Click **Format** menu.. `Alt`+`O`

continued...

FORMAT TABS COMMAND (CONTINUED)

2. Click **Tabs** .... ⊞T⊞

The Tabs dialog box displays.

3. Click **Default Tab Stops** scroll box .... Alt + F

4. Type number .... *number*
    for default tab stop.

5. Click ⎡ **OK** ⎤ .... ⏎

Ruler

> *NOTE: In order to set tab leaders or change
> default tab stops, it is necessary to use the
> **Format Tabs** command (see above).*

SET TAB STOPS

1. Select paragraphs for which you want to set tab stops.

2. Click **Tab Alignment** button at far left of horizontal ruler
    until desired tab stop button is visible:

    - Left-aligned tab stop .... 🄻

    - Center tab stop .... 🄻

    - Right-aligned tab stop .... 🄻

    - Decimal tab stop .... 🄻

3. Point mouse at desired tab stop position in horizontal
    ruler.

4. Click left mouse button to set tab.

5. Repeat steps 2 through 4 to set additional tab stops for
    selected paragraphs.

REMOVE TAB STOPS

1. Select paragraphs from which you want to remove tab stops.

2. Position mouse over tab stop you want to remove in horizontal ruler.

3. Hold left mouse button.

4. Drag mouse down to pull tab off ruler.

5. Release mouse button.

6. Repeat steps 2 through 5 to delete additional tab stops for selected paragraphs.

TABLES

COLUMN WIDTH AND
SPACE BETWEEN COLUMNS

Cell Height and Width Command

1. Select column or cell, or group of columns or cells you want to change.

2. Double-click column marker in horizontal ruler.

   OR

   a. Click **Ta**ble menu .... `Alt`+`A`

   b. Click **Cell Height and Width**............................. `W`

   The Cell Height and Width dialog box displays.

3. Click **Column** tab .... `←` `→`

4. Click **Width of Columns** text box .... `Alt`+`W`

   The name of the Width of Column text box changes to display the numbers of the selected columns (e.g., Width of Columns 1-2).

5. Type number .... *number* for column width.

   NOTE: To automatically adjust the width of the selected columns to fit the page margins, type "**Auto**".

   To automatically adjust width of selected columns according to their contents:

   Click [**AutoFit**] .... `Alt`+`A`

   NOTE: Selecting this command closes the **Cell Height and Width** dialog box.

6. Click **Space Between Columns** text box .... `Alt`+`S`

7. Type number .... *number* for space between columns.

8. Click [**OK**] .... `↵`

Mouse

1. Select column or cell, or group of columns or cells you want to change.

2. Point at column gridline to right of selected columns or cells.

Mouse changes to a ◆‖◆

   OR

   Point at table column marker in horizontal ruler above vertical gridline to right of selected columns or cells.

Mouse changes to a double-headed arrow.

3. Hold left mouse button.

4. Drag to new position and release mouse button.

Whether you drag column gridlines or column markers in the ruler, the following procedures apply:

- *Dragging the mouse by itself causes only selected columns or cells to resize.*

- *Holding down **Shift** while dragging proportionally adjusts only columns or cells immediately to right of selected columns or cells.*

- *Holding down **Ctrl** while dragging proportionally adjusts all columns and cells to right of selected columns or cells.*

- *Holding **Shift+Ctrl** adjusts selected columns or cells without changing other column or cell widths (table width changes).*

To automatically adjust width of selected columns or cells according to their contents:

1. Point at column gridline to right of selected columns or cells.

Mouse changes to a ◆‖◆

2. Double-click left mouse button.

CONVERT TABLE TO TEXT

1. Select table or rows within table you want to convert to paragraphs.

2. Click **Ta̲ble** menu.. `Alt` + `A`

3. Click **Con̲vert Table to Text** .... `V`

The Convert Table to Text dialog box displays.

4. Choose one of the following column separator options:

   • **P̲aragraphs**... `Alt` + `P`

   • **T̲abs**.. `Alt` + `T`

   • **Co̲mmas** .... `Alt` + `M`

   • **O̲ther**.. `Alt` + `O`

   Type character.. *character*

5. Click `OK` .... `↵`

CONVERT TEXT TO TABLES

Converts existing paragraphs to tables, allowing you to determine the number of columns and rows, column widths, and column separator characters.

> NOTE: *In addition to the following steps, you can also quickly convert text to tables by selecting the desired information and clicking on the* **Insert Table** *button in the* **Standard** *toolbar or by selecting* **Insert Table** *from the* **Table** *menu. Word automatically decides where to insert columns and rows into the selected text.*

1. Select paragraphs you want to convert to a table.

2. Click **Ta̲ble** menu.. `Alt` + `A`

3. Click **Con̲vert Text to Table** .... `V`

continued...

CONVERT TEXT TO TABLE (CONTINUED)

The Convert Text to Table dialog box displays.

To convert text to tables using the Table Wizard:

Click [**Wi̱zard...**] .... `Alt`+`Z`

*(See **Table Wizard**, page 149, for more information.)*

4. Click **Number of C̲olumns** text box .... `Alt`+`C`

5. Type number....................................... *number* of desired columns.

   NOTE: *Word selects the most logical number of columns based on the selected information.*

6. Click **Number of R̲ows** text box.................... `Alt`+`R`

7. Type number....................................... *number* of rows

   NOTE: *Word selects the most logical number of rows based on the selected information.*

8. Click **Column W̲idth** text box........................ `Alt`+`W`

9. Type number....................................... *number* for column width (default is **Auto**).

10. Choose one of the following options in the **Separate Text At** option box:

    • **P̲aragraphs**.. `Alt`+`P`

    • **T̲abs**.. `Alt`+`T`

    • **Co̲mmas**... `Alt`+`M`

    • **O̲ther**.. `Alt`+`O`

       Type character ....*character*

continued...

CONVERT TEXT TO TABLE (CONTINUED)

11. Click [AutoFormat...] .... Alt + A
    to automatically apply formatting to the
    new table. *(See **TABLE AUTOFORMAT**, page 160,
    for more information.)*

12. Click [OK] .... ↵

DELETE CELLS, ROWS, AND COLUMNS

Cells

1. Select cell or group of cells you want to delete.

2. Click **Table** menu .... Alt + A

3. Click **Delete Cells** .... D

The Delete Cells dialog box displays.

4. Choose one of the following options to delete cells:

    • Shift Cells **L**eft .... Alt + L

    • Shift Cells **U**p .... Alt + U

    • Delete Entire **R**ow .... Alt + R

    • Delete Entire **C**olumn .... Alt + C

5. Click [OK] .... ↵

Rows

1. Select row or group of rows you want to delete.

2. Click **Cut** button .... ✂
    in **Standard** toolbar.

    OR

continued...

a. Click **Ta̲ble** menu.. `Alt`+`A`

b. Click **D̲elete Rows** .... `D`

OR

a. Click **E̲dit** menu....................................... `Alt`+`E`

b. Click **Cu̲t** .... `T`

OR

Press **Ctrl+X**.. `Ctrl`+`X`

OR

Press **Shift+Delete** .... `Shift`+`Del`

Columns

1. Select columns or group of columns you want to delete.

2. Click **Cut** button .... `✄`
   in **Standard** toolbar.

   OR

   a. Click **Ta̲ble** menu................................. `Alt`+`A`

   b. Click **D̲elete Columns**........................... `D`

   OR

   a. Click **E̲dit** menu.................................... `Alt`+`E`

   b. Click **Cu̲t** .... `T`

   OR

   Press **Ctrl+X**.. `Ctrl`+`X`

   OR

   Press **Shift+Delete** .... `Shift`+`Del`

144

DISPLAY GRIDLINES

*NOTES: Table gridlines do not print. If you want to print lines between columns and rows of a table, it is necessary to apply a border. (See **BORDERS AND SHADING**, page 65, for more information.)*

This command toggles the display of gridlines for all tables within the active document.

1. Click T**a**ble menu..

2. Click Grid**l**ines...

FORMULA

Inserts formulas into a table as fields that perform mathematical calculations using cell references. Cell references are referred to as A1, A2, B1, B2, etc., with the letter representing the column, and the number representing the row. Formulas consist of an equals sign, followed by a specific function, then parenthesis containing the cell range (e.g., =SUM(A1:C5).

Cell ranges in formulas are referenced as follows:

Column Calculations   *Cell ranges are referred to as ABOVE or BELOW, depending on the location of the cursor. For example, "=SUM(ABOVE)" adds all cells above the cursor.*

Row Calculations   *Cell ranges are referred to as LEFT or RIGHT, depending on the location of the cursor. For example, "=SUM(LEFT)" adds all cells to the left of the cursor.*

Contiguous Ranges   *Type starting and ending cells, separated by a colon. For example, "=SUM(A1:C5)" adds all cells between cells A1 and C5.*

Non-Contiguous Ranges   *Type desired cell references, separated by commas. For example, "=SUM(A1,B2)" adds cells A1 and B2.*

continued...

FORMULA (CONTINUED)

*The default calculation for a table is addition (the SUM function). If you select the **Formula** command when your cursor is in a table, Word evaluates the location of the cursor and attempts to calculate the most logical cell range using the SUM function.*

*Formulas can also be inserted outside a table using numbers, bookmarks, and fields resulting in numbers. (See **FIELDS**, page 88, for more information.)*

1. Place cursor in table where you want to insert a formula.

2. Click **Table** menu .... `Alt`+`A`

3. Click **Formula** .... `O`

*The **Formula** dialog box displays.*

4. Type formula and cell range .... *text* into **Formula** text box.

   OR

   a. Click **Paste Function** .... `Alt`+`U` drop-down list box.

   b. Click function.

   c. Type cell range .... *text*

   To paste bookmark containing number reference into formula:

   a. Place cursor between parentheses of formula in **Formula** text box.

   b. Click **Paste Bookmark** .... `Alt`+`B` drop-down list box.

   *NOTE: The **Paste Bookmark** drop-down list box is not available if you do not have any bookmarks defined in your document.*

   c. Click bookmark .... `↑` `↓`

5. Click **Number Format** drop-down list box ..... `Alt`+`N`

continued...

146

FORMULA (CONTINUED)

6. Click number format .... ⬆️ ⬇️

    NOTE: If the numbers you are calculating include
    a number format (such as a percentage),
    the formula result automatically includes
    that format.

7. Click [**OK**] .... ↵

HEADINGS

Automatically repeats and updates table headings for tables spanning
more than one page.

> *NOTE: Table headings are not repeated or*
> *updated if a hard page break has been*
> *inserted into the table.*

1. Select rows you want to use as table headings.

2. Click **Ta**ble .... Alt + A

3. Click **H**eadings .... H

INSERT CELLS, ROWS, AND COLUMNS

Cells

1. Select a cell or group of cells.

    NOTE: The number of selected cells will be the
    number of new cells added.

2. Click **Insert Cells** button .... 🖽
    in **Standard** toolbar.

    OR

    a. Click **Ta**ble menu .... Alt + A

    b. Click **I**nsert Cells I

The Insert Cells dialog box displays.

continued...

3. Choose how to insert new cells from the following options:

- Shift Cells Right..............................`Alt`+`I`

- Shift Cells Down..............................`Alt`+`D`

- Insert Entire Row.............................`Alt`+`R`

- Insert Entire Column ....`Alt`+`C`

4. Click [**OK**] ....`↵`

Rows

1. Select a row or group of rows.

    NOTES: The number of selected rows will be the number of new rows added.

    New rows are inserted above the selected rows.

2. Click **Insert Rows** button..................................... 🔲
    in **Standard** toolbar.

    OR

    a. Click **Table** menu....................................`Alt`+`A`

    b. Click **Insert Rows** ....`I`

OR

1. Place cursor outside last cell in row.

    A new row is inserted above the active row.

2. Press **ENTER**...`↵`

    To insert new row at end of table:

    a. Place cursor in last cell of last row.

    b. Press **Tab** ....`Tab`

Columns

1. Select a column or group of rows

   *NOTE: The number of selected columns will be
   the number of new column added.*

New columns are inserted to the left of the selected columns.

2. Click **Insert Columns** button .... 🖬

   in **Standard** toolbar.

   OR

   a. Click **Table** menu .... Alt + A

   b. Click **Insert Columns** I

   To insert new column to right of table:

   a. Place cursor in cell outside last column.

   b. Click **Table** menu .... Alt + A

   c. Click **Select Column** C

   d. Repeat step 2.

INSERT TABLE

Insert Table Command

*Inserts a table using the **Insert Table** command, allowing you to
specify column widths and apply **AutoFormats**. This command also
allows you to select the **Table Wizard** (see page 149).*

1. Place cursor at location in document where you want to
   insert table.

2. Click **Table** menu .... Alt + A

3. Click **Insert** Table I

The Insert Table dialog box displays.

4. Click **Number of Columns** text box .... Alt + C

5. Type number .... *number*
   of columns (default is **2**).

continued...

6. Click **Number of Rows** text box.....................`Alt`+`R`

7. Type number..*number*
    of rows (default is **2**).

8. Click **Column Width** text box.......................`Alt`+`W`

9. Type number..*number*
    for column width (default is **Auto**).

10. Click | **AutoFormat...** | ....`Alt`+`A`
    if you want to apply an **AutoFormat**
    to the table. *(See TABLE AUTOFORMAT, page 160,
    for more information.)*

11. Click | **OK** | ....`↵`

Table Wizard

*Table Wizard is an automated routine that assists in creating
formatted tables.*

1. Place cursor at location in document where you want to
    insert table.

2. Click **Table** menu...`Alt`+`A`

3. Click **Insert** Table..`I`

The Insert Table dialog box displays.

4. Click | **Wizard...** | ....`Alt`+`Z`

The Table Wizard dialog box displays.

continued...

TABLE WIZARD (CONTINUED)

> *NOTE:* *The following commands are available in several of the **Table Wizard** steps:*

- | **<Back** | .... | Alt + B |

  to return to previous step.

- | **Next>** | .... | Alt + N |

- | **Finish** | .... | Alt + F |

  to skip following steps
  and immediately create table.

5. Choose one of the following table layout options:

   - Style 1 .... Alt + 1
   - Style 2 .... Alt + 2
   - Style 3 .... Alt + 3
   - Style 4 .... Alt + 4
   - Style 5 .... Alt + 5
   - Style 6 .... Alt + 6

6. Click **Next>** .... Alt + N

7. Choose one of the following column headings options:

   - **No headings, just _____ columns** .... Alt + H
     Type number .... *number*
     of columns.

   - **Months of the year** .... Alt + M
   - **Quarters (Q1, Q2, Q3, Q4)** .... Alt + Q
   - **Days of the week** .... Alt + D

continued...

TABLE WIZARD (CONTINUED)

- **Numbers, from ___ to ___** .... `Alt`+`R`

  then `Alt`+`T`

  Type desired numbers .... *numbers*

- **Years, from ____ to ___** .... `Alt`+`Y`

  then `Alt`+`O`

  Type desired years.................................... *years*

8. Click `Next>` .... `Alt`+`N`
9. Select type of row headings:

   - **No headings, just _____ columns** .... `Alt`+`H`
     Type number of columns............................ *number*

   - **Months of the year** .... `Alt`+`M`

   - **Quarters (Q1, Q2, Q3, Q4)** .... `Alt`+`Q`

   - **Days of the week** .... `Alt`+`D`

   - **Numbers, from ___ to ___** .... `Alt`+`R`

     then `Alt`+`T`

     Type desired numbers .... *numbers*

   - **Years, from ____ to ___** .... `Alt`+`Y`

     then `Alt`+`O`

     Type desired years.................................... *years*

10. Click `Next>` .... `Alt`+`N`
11. Choose information table cells will contain from the
    following options:

    - Numbers: right-aligned .... `Alt`+`R`

    - Numbers: aligned on decimal................... `Alt`+`D`

    - Text: left-aligned.................................... `Alt`+`L`

    - Text: centered.. `Alt`+`C`

continued...

TABLE WIZARD (CONTINUED)

12. Click **Next>** .... `Alt` + `N`

13. Choose one of the following orientation options:

- Portrait.. `Alt` + `P`

- Landscape... `Alt` + `L`

    *NOTE: If selected orientation is different from the
    orientation of the current page, the table is
    created on a new page.*

14. Click **Finish** .... `Alt` + `F`

    The Table AutoFormat dialog box displays.

15. Choose formatting options. *(See **TABLE AUTOFORMAT**,
    page 160, for more information.)*

16 Click **OK** .... `↵`

Insert Table Button

1.   Place cursor at location in document where you want to
     insert table.

2.   Click **Insert Table** button .... ▦
     in **Standard** toolbar.

*A grid displays that is used for selecting the desired number of rows
and columns.*

3.   Hold left mouse button.

4.   Drag over sizing grid to select desired number of rows
     and columns.

5.   Release mouse button.

MERGE CELLS

Merges two or more horizontally adjacent cells into one cell. When cells are merged together, the contents of each cell are converted to paragraphs within the combined cell.

1. Select cells you want to merge.

2. Click **Table** menu .... `Alt` + `A`

3. Click **Merge** Cells....... .. .. `M`

NAVIGATE IN TABLE

In addition to being able to point and click to move to different parts of a table, the following key combinations are available:

Next Cell.. `Tab`

Previous Cell... `Shift` + `Tab`

Right One Character... `→`

Left One Character.......... .... `←`

One Row Up........ .... `↑`

One Row Down.............. .... `↓`

First Cell in Current Row.................... `Alt` + `Home`

Last Cell in Current Row .... `Alt` + `End`

First Cell in Current Column .... `Alt` + `Page Up`

Last Cell in Current Column........................... `Alt` + `Page Down`

ROW HEIGHT AND ALIGNMENT

Changes the vertical height of rows and how they are aligned horizontally on a page. Also determines whether or not to allow page breaks to occur within a row.

1. Select row or group of rows whose height and alignment you want to change.

2. Double-click column marker horizontal ruler.

    OR

    a. Click **Table** menu .... `Alt`+`A`

    b. Click **Cell Height and Width** .... `W`

    The Cell Height and Width dialog box displays.

3. Click **Row** tab .... `←` `→`

4. Click **Height of Rows** drop-down list box ...... `Alt`+`E`

    The name of the Height of Rows drop-down list box changes to display the numbers of the selected rows (e.g., Height of Rows 1-2).

5. Click desired row height .... `↑` `↓`

    If you selected At Least or Exactly:

    a. Click **At** text box .... `Alt`+`A`

    b. Type number .... *number* for row height.

6. Click **Indent From Left** text box .... `Alt`+`F` if you wish to indent the selected rows.

7. Type number .... *number* for row indent.

8. Choose **Alignment** from the following options:

    *   Left .... `Alt`+`.L`

    *   Center .... `Alt`+`T`

    *   Right .... `Alt`+`I`

continued...

ROW HEIGHT AND ALIGNMENT (CONTINUED)

If you want to allow page breaks to occur within rows:

Click **Allow Row to Break Across Pages** ...... `Alt`+`B`
check box.

To change row height and alignment for other rows:

a. Click `Previous Row` .... `Alt`+`P`

   OR

   Click `Next Row` .... `Alt`+`N`

b. Repeats steps 4 through 8.

9. Click `OK` .... `↵`

Mouse

*Changes row heights using the mouse when in **Page Layout View**. (See **PAGE LAYOUT VIEW**, page 57, for more information.)*

1. Select row you want to change.

2. Point at table column marker in vertical ruler to left of selected row.

Mouse changes to a double-headed arrow.

3. Hold left mouse button.

4. Drag to new position and release mouse button.

SELECT IN TABLE

*(Also see **SELECT INFORMATION**, page 19, for information on selecting in other parts of a document.)*

Cells

Click left mouse button in cell's selection bar.

OR

Press **Tab** or **Shift+Tab** .... `Tab` or `Shift`+`Tab`
until desired cell is selected.

Rows

Click left mouse button in selection bar to left of row.
OR
1. Place cursor in row you want to select.

2. Click **Ta̲ble** menu .... `Alt`+`A`

3. Click **Select R̲ow** .... `R`

Columns

1. Position mouse above column until it changes to a down arrow.
2. Click left mouse button.
OR

1. Hold **Alt** key .... `Alt`
2. Click left mouse button.
OR
1. Place cursor in column you want to select.

2. Click **Ta̲ble** menu .... `Alt`+`A`

3. Click **Select C̲olumn** .... `C`

Entire Table

1. Place cursor in table you want to select.

2. a. Click **Ta̲ble** menu .... `Alt`+`A`

   b. Click **Select T̲able** .... `A`
   OR

   Press **Alt+NumPad 5** .... `Alt`+`5` *(NumPad)*
   NOTE: **Num Lock** key must be turned on.

SORT

1. Select information you want to sort (table rows or paragraphs).

2. Click **Ta̲ble** menu .... `Alt` + `A`

3. Click **Sor̲t** .... `T`

   NOTE: *The name of the **Sort** command changes between **Sort** if table rows are selected, or **Sort Text** if paragraphs are selected.*

The Sort dialog box displays.

4. Choose first tier sort options from the following:

   a. Click **S̲ort By** drop-down list box .... `Alt` + `S`

   b. Click first item by which to sort (e.g., column number, paragraph, field number, or name).

   NOTE: *Choices vary depending on selected information.*

   c. Click **Ty̲pe** drop-down list box .... `Alt` + `Y`

   d. Click desired sort option .... `'` or `"`

   e. Choose sort direction from the following options:

   - A̲scending .... `Alt` + `A`

   - D̲escending .... `Alt` + `D`

5. Choose second tier sort options.

   NOTE: *Options may not be available depending on choices made in step 4.*

   a. Click **T̲hen By** drop-down list box .... `Alt` + `T`

   b. Click second item by which to sort (e.g., column number, paragraph, field number, or name).

   NOTE: *Choices vary depending on selected information.*

continued...

158

  c. Click **Type** drop-down list box .... `Alt`+`P`

  d. Click how to sort information .... `↑` `↓`

  e. Choose sort direction from the following options:

-   Ascending .... `Alt`+`C`

-   Descending .... `Alt`+`N`

6. Choose third tier sort options.

   NOTE: Options may not be available depending on choices made in steps 4 and 5.

  a. Click **Then By** drop-down list box .... `Alt`+`B`

  b. Click third item by which to sort (e.g., column number, paragraph, field number, or name).

   NOTE: Choices vary depending on selected information.

  c. Click **Type** drop-down list box .... `Alt`+`E`

  d. Click how to sort information .... `↑` `↓`

  e. Choose sort direction from the following options:

-   Ascending .... `Alt`+`I`

-   Descending .... `Alt`+`G`

7. Choose one of the following **My List Has** options:

   NOTE: This option is available only if a table was selected in step 1.

-   Header Row .... `Alt`+`R`

-   No Header Row .... `Alt`+`W`

continued...

159

To access additional sort options:

Click [Options...] .... **Alt** + **O**

8. Click [OK] .... **↵**
   to begin sort.

SPLIT CELLS SPLIT CELLS

1. Select cell or group of cells you want to split.

2. Click **Table** menu .... **Alt** + **A**

3. Click **Split Cells** .... **P**

The Split Cells dialog box displays.

4. Type number.. *number*
   in **Number of Columns** text box.

   *NOTE: Each selected cell is split into the number
   of cells selected in the **Number of Columns**
   text box.*

5. Click [OK] .... **↵**

SPLIT TABLE

1. Place cursor in row where you want to start a new table.

2. a. Click **Table** menu...................................... **Alt** + **A**

   b. Click **Split** Table.. **S**

   OR

   Press **Shift+Ctrl+Enter** .... **Shift** + **Ctrl** + **↵**

   *NOTE: Delete the paragraph mark between two
   tables to remove a split.*

160

TABLE AUTOFORMAT

(Also see AUTOFORMAT, page 131, for information on applying automatic formatting to other sections of a document.)

1. Place cursor in table to which you want to apply automatic formatting.

2. Click **Ta̲ble** menu .... `Alt` + `A`

3. Click **Table AutoF̲ormat** .... `F`

    The Table AutoFormat dialog box displays.

4. Click **Forma̲ts** list box .... `Alt` + `T`

5. Click format .... `↑` `↓`

6. Choose from the following **Formats to Apply** options:

    *   B̲orders .... `Alt` + `B`

    *   S̲hading .... `Alt` + `S`

    *   F̲ont .... `Alt` + `F`

    *   C̲olor .... `Alt` + `C`

    *   AutoF̲it .... `Alt` + `I`

7. Choose from the following **Apply Special Formats To** options:

    *   Headings R̲ows .... `Alt` + `R`

    *   First C̲olumn .... `Alt` + `O`

    *   L̲ast Row .... `Alt` + `L`

    *   Last Col̲umn .... `Alt` + `U`

8. Click `  OK  ` .... `↵`

TABS IN CELLS

*(See **TABS**, page 133, for more information.)*

1. Place cursor in cell where you want to insert a tab character.

2. Press **Ctrl+Tab**..

> NOTE: *Word automatically aligns numbers and other information contained in a cell if it is formatted with a single **decimal tab** (but not other types of tabs). Therefore, it is not necessary to insert a tab character if a single decimal tab is set in a cell references.*

162

REFERENCES

BOOKMARKS

*Bookmarks are used for marking the location of information in a document. You can select to view bookmarks in your document with the **View** tab under **Tools Options**. (See **VIEW OPTIONS**, page 275, for more information.)*

Define

1. Select information or place cursor at location in document where you want to create bookmark.

2. a. Click **Edit** menu .... `Alt`+`E`

    b. Click **Bookmark** .... `B`

    OR

    Press **Shift+Ctrl+F5** .... `Shift`+`Ctrl`+`F5`

*The **Bookmark** dialog box displays.*

3. Click **Bookmark Name** text box................ `Alt`+`B`

4. Type name...*name*
    for new bookmark.

    OR

    Type or click bookmark name............ *name* or `↑` `↓`
    to redefine existing bookmark.

5. Click [**Add**] .... `Alt`+`A`

Delete

> NOTE: You can also delete a bookmark by deleting the information it represents.

1. a. Click **Edit** menu .... `Alt`+`E`

    b. Click **Bookmark** .... `B`

    OR

    Press **Shift+Ctrl+F5** .... `Shift`+`Ctrl`+`F5`

continued…

163

The Bookmark dialog box displays.

2. Click **B**ookmark Name text box...................... Alt + B

3. Type or Click bookmark name............ *name* or ↑ ↓
   you want to delete.

4. Click | **Delete** | .... Alt + D

Go To

> NOTE: *You can also jump to a bookmark using the **Go To** command. (See **NAVIGATE**, page 13, for more information.)*

1. a. Click **E**dit menu....................................... Alt + E

   b. Click **B**ookmark .... B

   OR

   Press **Shift+Ctrl+F5** .... Shift + Ctrl + F5

The Bookmark dialog box displays.

2. Double-click bookmark to which you want to move.

   OR

   a. Click **B**ookmark Name text box .... Alt + B

   b. Type or Click bookmark name ...... *name* or ↑ ↓

   c. Click | **Go To** | .... Alt + G

3. Click | **Close** | .... Esc

CAPTIONS

*Numbered captions, created with **SEQ** fields, can be added to graphics, tables, and other information in a document. Numbered captions can be easily updated if a caption is moved, copied, or deleted. (See **FIELDS**, page 88, for information on updating and working with fields.)*

Insert Caption

1. Click item for which you want to add a caption.

2. Click **Insert** menu.................................... `Alt`+`I`

3. Click **Caption** .... `I`

*The **Caption** dialog box displays.*

4. Click **Label** drop-down list box.................. `Alt`+`L`

5. Click label name..................................... `↑` `↓`

   To create new label name:

   a. Click **New Label...** .... `Alt`+`N`

   *The **New Label** dialog box displays.*

   b. Type name...................................... *name*
      for new label.

   c. Click **OK** .... `↵`

   To delete label name:

   a. Click **Label** drop-down list box............. `Alt`+`L`

   b. Click label name .... `↑` `↓`
      you want to delete.

   c. Click **Delete Label** .... `Alt`+`D`

   NOTE: *You cannot delete default labels (**Figure**, **Table**, **Equation**).*

continued...

6. Click **Caption** text box .... `Alt`+`C`

7. Type text .... *text*
   for caption (defaults to label name selected in step 5,
   followed by a number).

   To change caption's numbering format:

   Click [**Numbering...**] .... `Alt`+`U`

8. Click **Position** drop-down list box .... `Alt`+`P`

   NOTE: The **Position** drop-down list box is
   unavailable if no item was selected in
   step 1.

9. Choose label position from the following options:

   • Above Selected Item .... `↑` `↓`

   • Below Selected Item .... `↑` `↓`

10. Click [**OK**] .... `↵`

AutoCaption

Automatically inserts a caption when a selected item is inserted into a
document.

1. Click **Insert** menu .... `Alt`+`I`

2. Click **Caption** .... `I`

   The Caption dialog box displays.

3. Click [**AutoCaption...**] .... `Alt`+`A`

   The AutoCaption dialog box displays.

4. Click **Add Caption When Inserting** list box ... `Alt`+`A`

continued...

166

AUTOCAPTION (CONTINUED)

5. Click item.................................... ⬆️ ⬇️ then Space
   for which you want to
   automatically insert captions.

6. Click **Use Label** drop-down list box.............. Alt + L

7. Click label name.. ⬆️ ⬇️

   To create new label name:

   a. Click [**New Label...**] .... Alt + N

   The New Label dialog box displays.

   b. Type name..*name*
      for new label.

   c. Click [**OK**] .... ⏎

   NOTE: *To delete a label, it is necessary to use the*
   *   **Insert Caption** command, above.*

8. Click **Position** drop-down list box................. Alt + P

   NOTE: *The **Position** drop-down list box is*
   *   unavailable if no item was selected in*
   *   step 1.*

9. Choose label position from the following options:

   • Above Item.. ⬆️ ⬇️

   • Below Item.. ⬆️ ⬇️

   To change AutoCaption numbering format:

   Click [**Numbering...**] .... Alt + U

10. Click [**OK**] .... ⏎

CROSS-REFERENCES

Cross-references in Word, created with REF fields, can refer to footnotes, endnotes, bookmarks, captions, or paragraphs created using heading styles. (See FIELDS, page 88, for information on updating and working with fields.)

1. Place cursor in document where you want to insert a cross-reference.

2. Click **Insert** menu .... `Alt`+`I`

3. Click **Cross-reference** .... `R`

The Cross-reference dialog box displays.

> NOTE: The choices in the **Cross-reference** dialog box vary depending on the available references items in the active document.

4. Click **Reference Type** list box .... `Alt`+`T`

5. Click desired reference type .... `↑` `↓`

6. Click **Insert Reference To** list box................. `Alt`+`R`

7. Click type of information .... `↑` `↓`
   to which you want to refer.

> NOTE: Choices vary depending on option selected in step 5.

8. Click **For Which** list box .... `Alt`+`W`

9. Click specific item .... `↑` `↓`
   to which you want to refer .

> NOTE: Choices vary depending on option selected in step 5.

10. Click [**Insert**] .... `Alt`+`I`

11. Click [**Close**] .... `Esc`

FOOTNOTES/ENDNOTES

Insert

INSERT FOOTNOTE COMMAND

1. Place cursor in document where you want to insert a footnote or endnote.

2. Click **I**nsert menu.................................... `Alt`+`I`

3. Click Foot**n**ote .... `N`

    The Footnote and Endnote dialog box displays.

4. Choose type of note to insert from the following options:

    *   **F**ootnote.. `Alt`+`F`

    *   **E**ndnote.. `Alt`+`E`

5. Choose type of numbering from the following options:

    *   **A**utoNumber .... `Alt`+`A`

    *   **C**ustom Mark... `Alt`+`C`

        Type character...*text*

    To insert special character from Symbol dialog box:

    Click **S**ymbol... .... `Alt`+`S`

    *(See **Symbols**, page 84, for more information.)*

6. Click OK .... `↵`

    The Note pane displays.

7   Type text..*text*
    for footnote or endnote.

8. Click **C**lose .... `Shift`+`Alt`+`C`
    to close **Note** pane.

KEYBOARD

1. Place cursor in document where you want to insert footnote or endnote.

2. Press **Ctrl+Alt+F** .... Ctrl + Alt + F
   to insert footnote.

   OR

   Press **Ctrl+Alt+E** .... Ctrl + Alt + E
   to insert endnote.

   NOTE: *If the last footnote or endnote inserted into the document used the **AutoNumber** format, the next consecutive **AutoNumber** footnote or endnote is inserted. If the last footnote or endnote inserted into the document used a custom mark, the **Footnote and Endnote** dialog box displays.*

   The Note pane displays.

3. Type text .... *text*
   for footnote or endnote.

4. Click [Close] .... Shift + Alt + C
   to close **Note** pane.

Display/Edit

*Displays the **Note** pane and allows you to edit footnotes and endnotes in a document. You can also display and edit footnotes and endnotes when in **Print Preview** or **Page Layout View**.*

   NOTE: *You can jump to a footnote or endnote using the **Go To** command. (See **NAVIGATE**, page 13, for more information.)*

1. Double-click footnote or endnote mark in document.

   OR

   a. Click **View** menu .... Alt + V

continued . .

170

DISPLAY/EDIT (CONTINUED)

 b. Click **Footnotes** .... **F**

The Note pane displays.

2. Click **Notes** drop-down list box .... **Shift** + **Alt** + **N**

3. Choose type of notes to display:

 • All Footnotes .... **↑** **↓**

 • All Endnotes .... **↑** **↓**

 NOTE: *Both choices, **All Footnotes** or **All**
 ***Endnotes** are only available if a footnote or
 an endnote, respectively, has already been
 inserted into the document.*

4. Make desired changes to footnotes or endnotes.

5. Click **Close** .... **Shift** + **Alt** + **C**
 to close **Note** pane.

Delete

1. Select footnote or endnote mark in document
 representing the footnote or endnote you want to delete.

2. a. Click **Edit** menu .... **Alt** + **E**

 b. Click **Clear** .... **A**
 OR

 Press **Delete** .... **Del**
 OR

 Press **Backspace** .... **Backspace**

Options

ALL FOOTNOTES

1. Click **Insert** menu .... `Alt`+`I`

2. Click **Footnote** .... `N`

The Footnote and Endnote dialog box displays.

3. Click [**Options...**] .... `Alt`+`O`

The Note Options dialog box displays.

4. Click **All Footnotes** tab .... `Alt`+`F`

5. Click **Place At** drop-down list box .... `Alt`+`P`

6. Choose where to place footnotes from the following options:

   - Bottom of Page .... `↑` `↓`

   - Beneath Text .... `↑` `↓`

7. Click **Number Format** drop-down list box ..... `Alt`+`N`

8. Click footnote number format .... `↑` `↓`

9. Click **Start At** scroll box .... `Alt`+`A`

10. Type starting number .... *number*

11. Choose **Numbering** option from the following:

    - Continuous .... `Alt`+`C`

    - Restart Each Section .... `Alt`+`S`

    - Restart Each Page .... `Alt`+`G`

12. Click [**OK**] .... `↵`

172

ALL ENDNOTES

1. Click <u>I</u>nsert menu... `Alt`+`I`

2. Click Foot<u>n</u>ote .... `N`

The Footnote and Endnote dialog box displays.

3. Click [<u>O</u>ptions...] .... `Alt`+`O`

The Note Options dialog box displays.

4. Click All <u>E</u>ndnotes tab................................. `Alt`+`E`

5. Click <u>P</u>lace At drop-down list box................. `Alt`+`P`

6. Choose where to place endnotes from the following options:

   - End of Section... `↑` `↓`

   - End of Document .... `↑` `↓`

7. Click <u>N</u>umber Format drop-down list box..... `Alt`+`N`

8. Click number format for endnotes .... `↑` `↓`

9. Click Start <u>A</u>t scroll box .... `Alt`+`A`

10. Type starting number .... *number*

11. Choose **Numbering** option from the following:

    - <u>C</u>ontinuous .... `Alt`+`C`

    - Restart Each <u>S</u>ection................................. `Alt`+`S`

12. Click [OK] .... `↵`

CONVERT

Converts footnotes to endnotes and vice versa.

1. Click **Insert** menu .... `Alt`+`I`

2. Click **Footnote** .... `N`

The Footnote and Endnote dialog box displays.

3. Click **Options...** .... `Alt`+`O`

   NOTE: This option is unavailable if no footnotes or endnotes have been inserted into the active document.

The Note Options dialog box displays.

4. Click **Convert...** .... `Alt`+`T`
   from either **All Footnotes** or **All Endnotes** tabs.

The Convert Notes dialog box displays.

5. Choose one of the following options:

   • Convert All Footnotes to Endnotes .... `Alt`+`F`

   • Convert All Endnotes to Footnotes .... `Alt`+`E`

   • Swap Footnotes and Endnotes .... `Alt`+`S`

6. Click **OK** .... `↵`

Continuation Notices and Separators

Displays and allows you to change footnote and endnote separators, and continuation notices.

1. Double-click a footnote or endnote mark in document.

   OR

   a. Click **View** menu... **Alt** + **V**

   b. Click **Footnotes** .... **F**

   The Note pane displays.

2. Click **Notes** drop-down list box......... **Shift** + **Alt** + **N**

3. Choose type of notes whose separators and continuation notice you want to change:

   • All Footnotes... **↑** **↓**

   • All Endnotes.. **↑** **↓**

   NOTE: *Both choices, **All Footnotes** or **All Endnotes** are only available if a footnote or an endnote, respectively, has already been inserted into the document.*

4. Click **Notes** drop-down list box......... **Shift** + **Alt** + **N**

5. Click item you want to change .... **↑** **↓**

6. Make desired changes to selected item.

7. Click **Close** .... **Shift** + **Alt** + **C**
   to close **Note** pane.

INDEX AND TABLES

Indexes and information tables in Word are created using fields. (See FIELDS, page 88, for information on updating and working with fields.)

Index

Marks index entries and compiles an index in the current document.

MARK INDEX ENTRY

Creates index entries for compilation into an index.

1. Select information you want to use as index entry or position cursor in document where you want to insert index entry.

2. Press **Shift+Alt+X** .... `Shift`+`Alt`+`X`

   OR

   a. Click **Insert** menu .... `Alt`+`I`

   b. Click **Index and Tables** .... `X`

   *The **Index and Tables** dialog box displays.*

   c. Click **Index** tab .... `Alt`+`X`

   d. Click **Mark Entry...** .... `Alt`+`↵`

   *The **Mark Index Entry** dialog box displays.*

3. Click **Main Entry** text box .... `Alt`+`E`

4. Type text .... *text*
   you want to use for index entry.

   NOTE: *Any text selected in step 1 appears in the **Main Entry** text box.*

5. Click **Subentry** text box .... `Alt`+`S`

6. Type text .... *text*
   for subentry.

continued...

176

7. Choose one of the following options:

*   **Cross-reference** .... `Alt`+`C`

    Type text ....*text*
    to use for cross-reference.

    *NOTE: Cross-reference text can also be formatted
    using shortcut keys. (See **CHARACTER
    FORMAT**, page 78, for more information.*

*   **Current Page** .... `Alt`+`P`

*   **Page Range Bookmark**......................... `Alt`+`R`

    Click bookmark.. `↑` `↓`
    used to mark page range.

8. Choose one of the following **Page Number Format**
    options:

*   **Bold** .... `Alt`+`B`

*   **Italic**... `Alt`+`I`

9. Click [**Mark**] .... `Alt`+`M`
    to mark single occurrence of index entry.

    OR

    Click [**Mark All**] .... `Alt`+`A`
    to mark all occurrences of index entry in document.

    *NOTE: The **Mark All** button is only available if text
    was selected in step 1.*

10 Click [**Close**] .... `Esc`

CONCORDANCE FILE

Creates a concordance file, used for automatically marking index entries in a document with AutoMark (see below).

1. Create new file. *(See **NEW FILE**, page 34, for more information.)*

2. Insert two-column table. *(See **INSERT TABLE**, page 148, for more information.)*

3. In first column of table, type text you want Word to search for when creating index entries.

4. In second column of table, type index entries exactly as you want them to appear in index.

   NOTES: Entries in both columns of the table are case-sensitive. Create a new row for each index reference and entry.

   Instead of a table, concordance file entries can also be separated by tabs.

5. Save file. *(See **SAVE FILE**, page 43, for more information.)*

AUTOMARK

Creates index entries in the current document, from index entries contained in a concordance file (see above).

1. Click **Insert** menu .... `Alt`+`I`

2. Click **Index and Tables** .... `X`

   The Index and Tables dialog box displays.

3. Click **Index** tab .... `Alt`+`X`

4. Click [**AutoMark...**] .... `Alt`+`U`

   The Open Index AutoMark File dialog box displays.

5. Click **List Files of Type** drop-down list box... `Alt`+`T`

6. Click concordance file type................................. `↑` `↓`

continued...

178

7. Click **Dri̲ves** drop-down list box.................... `Alt`+`V`

8. Type or Click drive letter .... *drive* or `↑``↓`
    containing concordance file.

9. Double-click directory in **Directories** list box that
    contains concordance file.

    OR

    a. Click **D̲irectories** list box .... `Alt`+`D`

    b. Click directory .... `↑``↓`

    c. Press **ENTER** .... `↵`

10. Double-click concordance file in **File Name** list box.

    OR

    a. Click **File N̲ame** list box .... `Alt`+`N`

    b. Type file name .... *file name*

    c. Click [**OK**] .... `↵`

COMPILE INDEX

1. Place cursor in document where you want to insert
    index.

2. Click **I̲nsert** menu.............................. `Alt`+`I`

3. Click **Inde̲x and Tables** .... `X`

    The Index and Tables dialog box displays.

4. Click **Inde̲x** tab................................ `Alt`+`X`

5. Choose index type from the following options:

    • Inde̲nted................................ `Alt`+`D`

    • Ru̲n-in.................................. `Alt`+`N`

continued...

6. Click **Formats** list box .... `Alt`+`T`

7. Click desired index format........................ `↑` `↓`

   To create custom index format:

   a. Click **Formats** list box...................... `Alt`+`T`

   b. Click **From Template**........................ `↑` `↓`

   c. Click [**Modify...**] .... `Alt`+`M`

   *NOTE: This option is only available if **From Template** was selected in previous step.*

The Style dialog box displays. (See STYLES, page 123, for more information.)

8. Click **Right Align Page Numbers** .... `Alt`+`R`
   if desired.

   *NOTE: This option is unavailable if **Run-In** was selected in step 5.*

9. Click **Columns** scroll box .... `Alt`+`O`

10. Type number of columns .... *number*

11. Click **Tab Leader** drop-down list box........... `Alt`+`B`

    *NOTE: This option is unavailable if **Indented** was selected in step 5.*

12. Click tab leader.. `↑` `↓`

13. Click [**OK**] .... `↵`

Table of Contents

MARK TABLE OF CONTENTS ENTRY

Creates table entries for compilation into a table of contents.

1. Select information you want to use as table entry, or position cursor in document where you want to insert table entry.

2. Press **Shift+Alt+O** .... `Shift`+`Alt`+`O`

The Mark Table of Contents Entry dialog box displays.

3. Click **Entry** text box .... `Alt`+`E`

4. Type text you want to use for table entry. .... *text*

   NOTE: *Any text selected in step 1 appears in the* ***Entry*** *text box.*

5. Click **Table Identifier** drop-down list box ..... `Alt`+`I`

6. Click table identifier.............. .... `↑` `↓`

7. Click **Level** scroll box .... `Alt`+`L`

8. Type number for table level .... *number*

9. Click [**Mark**] .... `Alt`+`M`

COMPILE TABLE OF CONTENTS

Compiles a table of contents in the current document. By default, Word compiles a table of contents from heading styles, although you can also use other styles and table entry fields.

1. Place cursor in document where you want to insert table of contents.

2. Click **Insert** menu................. .... `Alt`+`I`

3. Click **Index and Tables**........ .... `X`

The Index and Tables dialog box displays.

4. Click **Table of Contents** tab .... `Alt`+`C`

continued...

TABLE OF CONTENTS (CONTINUED)

5. Click **Formats** list box .... `Alt`+`T`

6. Click desired table of contents format .... `↑` `↓`

   To create custom table of contents format:

   a. Click **Formats** list box .... `Alt`+`T`

   b. Click **From Template** .... `↑` `↓`

   c. Click [**Modify...**] .... `Alt`+`M`

   NOTE: *This option is only available if **From Template** was selected in previous step.*

The Style dialog box displays. (See STYLES, page 123, for more information.)

7. Choose from the following page number options:

   • **S**how Page Numbers .... `Alt`+`S`

   • **R**ight Align Page Numbers .... `Alt`+`R`

8. Click **Show Levels** scroll box .... `Alt`+`L`

9. Type number .... *number*
   for number of levels in table of contents.

10. Click **Tab Leader** drop-down list box .... `Alt`+`B`

11. Click tab leader .... `↑` `↓`

    To create table of contents with styles other than heading styles, or to include table entry fields:

    a. Click [**Options...**] .... `Alt`+`O`

The Table of Contents Options dialog box displays.

    b. Click **TOC Level** list box .... `Alt`+`L`

continued..

182

c. Click style .... `Tab`
   you want to use to compile table of contents.

d. Type number .... *number*
   for table of contents level.

NOTE: *Styles that have been selected to use for
        compiling the table of contents have a
        check mark next to them.*

e. Click **Table Entry Fields** .... `Alt`+`E`
   to include table entry fields
   when compiling table of contents.

f. Deselect **Styles** check box .... `Alt`+`S`
   to use only table entry fields
   when compiling table of contents.

**To restore Table of Contents dialog box settings to use
heading styles:**

Click `Reset` .... `Alt`+`R`

g. Click `OK` .... `↵`
   to close **Table of** Contents dialog box.

12. Click `OK` .... `↵`
    to compile table of contents.

Table of Figures

*Compile a table of figures from captions by default, although you can
also use styles and table entry fields. (See CAPTIONS, page 164, for
more information. Also see Mark Table Of Contents Entry, page
180.)*

1. Place cursor in document where you want to insert table
   of figures.

2. Click **Insert** menu .... `Alt`+`I`

continued...

TABLE OF FIGURES (CONTINUED)

3. Click **Index and Tables** X

The Index and Tables dialog box displays.

4. Click **Table of Figures** tab.......................... Alt + F

5. Click **Caption Label** list box .... Alt + L

6. Click caption label .... ↑ ↓
   to use when compiling table of figures.

   To create table of figures from a style, or to include table entry fields:

   a. Click | **Options...** | .... Alt + O

   The Table of Figures Options dialog box displays.

   b. Click **Style** check box............................. Alt + S
      to create table of figures from selected style.

   c. Click **Table Entry Fields** .... Alt + E
      to include table entry fields
      when compiling table of figures.

   d. Click **Table Identifier**........................... Alt + I
      to assign a letter to the table.

   e. Click identifier... ↑ ↓

   d. Click | **OK** | .... ↵

7. Click **Formats** list box .... Alt + T

8. Click desired table of figures format................. ↑ ↓

   To create custom table of contents format:

   a. Click **Formats** list box............................ Alt + T

   b. Click **From Template**............................... ↑ ↓

   c. Click | **Modify...** | .... Alt + M

continued...

TABLE OF FIGURES (CONTINUED)

> NOTE: This option is only available if **From Template** was selected in previous step.

*The **Style** dialog box displays. (See **STYLES**, page 123, for more information.)*

9. Choose from the following options:

- Show Page Numbers .... `Alt`+`S`

- Right Align Page Numbers .... `Alt`+`R`

- Include Label and Number .... `Alt`+`N`

10. Click **Tab Leader** drop-down list box............ `Alt`+`B`

11. Click tab leader .... `↑` `↓`

12. Click ` OK ` .... `↵`

Table of Authorities

Tables of Authorities are created using two types of citations: long citations and short citations. Long citations, in a legal document, are used only once and contain the entire text of the citation. Any further reference to the same source is called a short citation and contains a brief summary of the text contained in the associated long citation. Long citations must appear first in a document.

*Citations are created using **TA** fields. In order to edit the text of a citation, it is necessary to edit the hidden text contained in the field codes. (See **FIELDS**, page 88, for more information.)*

MARK CITATION

1. Select information you want to use as a long citation, or position cursor in document where you want to insert a citation entry.

2. Press **Shift+Alt+I** .... `Shift`+`Alt`+`I`

   OR

   a. Click **Insert** menu .... `Alt`+`I`

continued...

TABLE OF AUTHORITIES (CONTINUED)

b. Click **Inde<u>x</u> and Tables**................................. X

The Index and Tables dialog box displays.

c. Click **Table of <u>A</u>uthorities** tab................. Alt + A

d. Click [**Mar<u>k</u> Citation...**] .... Alt + K

NOTES: *The **Mark Citation** dialog box displays. Any
text selected in step 1 appears in both the
Selected Text and **Short Citation** text
boxes.*

*Citations entries in the **Mark Citations**
dialog box can be formatted using shortcut
keys. (See **CHARACTER FORMAT**, page
78, for more information.)*

3. Click **Selected <u>T</u>ext** text box .... Alt + T

4. Create or edit text for long citation.

5. Click **<u>C</u>ategory** drop-down list box................ Alt + C

6. Click citation category .... ↑ ↓

To modify citation category:

a. Click [**Category...**] .... Alt + G

The Edit Category dialog box displays.

b. Click **<u>C</u>ategory** list box............................ Alt + C

c. Click citation category............................... ↑ ↓
you want to modify.

d. Click **Replace <u>W</u>ith** text box .... Alt + W

e. Type replacement text.. *text*
for citation category.

continued...

TABLE OF AUTHORITIES (CONTINUED)

f. Click **Replace** .... `Alt`+`R`

g. Click **OK** .... `↵`
   to close **Edit Category** dialog box.

7. Click **Short Citation** text box .... `Alt`+`S`

8. Create or edit text for short citation.

9. Click **Mark** .... `Alt`+`M`
   to mark single occurrence of citation.

   OR

   Click **Mark All** .... `Alt`+`A`
   to mark all occurrences of short and long
   citation in document.

   To mark additional citations in the document:

   a. Click **Next Citation** .... `Alt`+`N`

   b. Repeat steps 3 through 9.

10. Click **Close** .... `Esc`

COMPILE TABLE OF AUTHORITIES

1. Place cursor in document where you want to insert table
   of authorities.

2. Click **Insert** menu .... `Alt`+`I`

3. Click **Index and Tables** .... `X`

   The Index and Tables dialog box displays.

4. Click **Table of Authorities** tab .... `Alt`+`A`

5. Click **Formats** list box .... `Alt`+`T`

6. Click desired table of authorities format .... `↑` `↓`

continued...

TABLE OF AUTHORITIES (CONTINUED)

To create custom table of authorities format:

a. Click **Forma̲ts** list box .... `Alt`+`T`

b. Click **From Template** .... `↑` `↓`

c. Click [Mo̲dify...] .... `Alt`+`M`

NOTE: *This option is only available if **From Template** was selected in previous step.*

*The **Style** dialog box displays. (See STYLES, page 123, for more information.)*

7. Choose from the following options:

   • Use P̲assim .... `Alt`+`P`

   • Keep Original Fo̲rmatting .... `Alt`+`R`

8. Click **Categ̲ory** drop-down list box .... `Alt`+`G`

9. Click category .... `↑` `↓`
   for which to compile citations.

10. Click **Ta̲b Leader** drop-down list box .... `Alt`+`B`

11. Click tab leader .... `↑` `↓`

12. Click [**OK**] .... `↵`

PROOFING TOOLS

ANNOTATIONS

Annotations are used for inserting comments into a document by different reviewers. Annotation marks appear in a document as hidden text, consisting of the reviewer's initials and a number.

Annotations can be printed with the document or by themselves. (See PRINT, page 17, for more information.)

Insert

1. Place cursor at position in document where you want to insert annotation.

2. a. Click **Insert** menu .... `Alt` + `I`

    b. Click **Annotation** .... `A`

    OR

    Press **Ctrl+Alt+A** .... `Ctrl` + `Alt` + `A`

    *NOTE: An annotation mark, consisting of the reviewer's intials and a number, is inserted and the **Annotations** pane displays.*

3. Type annotation text ....*text*

    To insert Sound object for annotation:

    Click **Insert Sound Object** button .... 🖭

    *NOTE: Sound objects are only available if sound equipment is installed in your computer. (See **EMBEDDED OBJECTS**, page 233, for more information.)*

4. Click `Close` .... `Shift` + `Alt` + `C`

    to close **Annotations** pane.

Display

> NOTE: You can jump to an annotation using the **Go To** command. (See **NAVIGATE**, page 13, for more information.)

1. Double-click annotation mark in document.

   OR

   a. Click **View** menu .... `Alt`+`V`

   b. Click **Annotations** .... `A`

   *The **Annotations** pane displays.*

2. Click **From** drop-down list box .... `Alt`+`R`

3. Click reviewer .... `↑` `↓`
   whose annotations you want displayed
   (default is **All Reviewers**).

4. Click `Close` .... `Shift`+`Alt`+`C`
   to close **Annotations** pane.

Delete

1. Select annotation mark in document representing annotation you want to delete.

2. a. Click **Edit** menu .... `Alt`+`E`

   b. Click **Clear** .... `A`

   OR

   Press **Delete** .... `F10`

   OR

   Press **Backspace** .... `Backspace`

AUTOCORRECT

Corrects mistakes in a document automatically as you type.

1. Place your cursor anywhere in document, or select text you want to use as an **AutoCorrect**.

2. Click **Tools** menu .... `Alt` + `T`

3. Click **AutoCorrect** .... `A`

The AutoCorrect dialog box displays.

4. Choose from the following **AutoCorrect** options:

   - Correct TWo INitial CApitals .... `Alt` + `C`

   - Capitalize First Letter of **S**entences .... `Alt` + `S`

   - Capitalize **N**ames of Days .... `Alt` + `N`

   - Correct accidental usage .... `Alt` + `L`
     of cAPS **L**OCK Key

   - Replace **T**ext As You Type .... `Alt` + `L`

   To add new AutoCorrect entry:

   a. Click **R**eplace text box .... `Alt` + `E`

   b. Type text .... *text*
      you want automatically replaced as you type.

   c. Click **W**ith text box .... `Alt` + `W`

   d. Type text .... *text*
      with which you want to replace text typed in step b.

   NOTE: *Any text selected in step 1 appears in the* ***With*** *dialog box.*

   e. Click **P**lain Text .... `Alt` + `P`
      OR

      Click **F**ormatted Text .... `Alt` + `F`

continued...

NOTE: *Plain Text* or *Formatted Text* options are
        only available if you selected text in step *1*.

f. Click [__A__dd] .... `Alt`+`A`

To delete existing AutoText entry:

a. Click **AutoText** entry .... `↑` `↓`
    you want to delete.

b. Click [__D__elete] .... `Alt`+`D`

To change existing AutoText entry:

a. Click **AutoText** entry .... `↑` `↓`
    you want to change.

b. Click **W**ith text box.............................. `Alt`+`W`

c. Type text.. *text*
    with which you want to replace
    AutoText entry selected in step b.

d. Click [Repl**a**ce] .... `Alt`+`A`

5. Click [**OK**] .... `↵`

GRAMMAR

NOTE: *Word also spell checks the document or
        selected text as it is performing a grammar
        check if the option is selected in the
        Grammar tab under Tools Options. (See
        SPELLING, page 203, and GRAMMAR
        OPTIONS, page 267, for more
        information.)*

1. Place cursor in document where you want to begin
    grammar check, or select text you want to grammar
    check.

continued...

GRAMMAR (CONTINUED)

2. Click **T**ools menu .... `Alt`+`T`

3. Click **G**rammar .... `G`

The Grammar dialog box displays.

> NOTE: *Word displays incorrect sentences in the* **Sentence** *list box. You can edit the sentence displayed. Suggested alternatives for the incorrect sentence are displayed in the* **Suggestions** *list box.*

To choose alternate grammar suggestion:

a. Click **Suggestions** list box .... `Alt`+`G`

b. Click grammar suggestion .... `↑` `↓`

4. Choose one of the following commands for each grammatical error:

- [**Ignore**] .... `Alt`+`I`

  to ignore grammatical error.

- [**N**ext Sentence] .... `Alt`+`N`

  to ignore all other errors in current sentence and move to next sentence with grammatical errors.

- [**C**hange] .... `Alt`+`C`

  to replace grammatical error with selection in **Suggestions** box.

- [**Ignore R**ule] .... `Alt`+`R`

  to ignore all other instances of grammatical error.

- [**E**xplain...] .... `Alt`+`E`

  to display explanation of why selected sentence is not grammatically correct.

continued...

- | **Options...** | `Alt` + `O`

  to access **Grammar** tab under **Tools Options**.
  *(See GRAMMAR OPTIONS, page 267, for more
  information.)*

- | **Undo Last** | `Alt` + `L`

  to reverse last action.

5. Click | **Cancel** | `Esc`

  to exit **Grammar** dialog box
  without making any changes.

  OR

  Click | **Close** | `Esc`

  to exit **Grammar** dialog box
  after making desired changes.

HIGHLIGHTER PEN

Marks selected text for emphasis or to note revisions.

1. Click **Highlight** icon...
   on Formatting toolbar.

2. Select information you want to highlight.

3. Click **Highlight** icon again or press **Esc**.............. `Esc`
   to turn off highlighting.

   To select a different highlighting color:

   a. Click drop-down arrow next to **Highlight** icon.

   b. Click desired color or hold left mouse button and
      drag cursor to lower right-hand corner of list box to
      display additional colors.

continued...

HIGHLIGHTER PEN (CONTINUED)
EXAMPLE OF HIGHLIGHTER COLORS LIST:

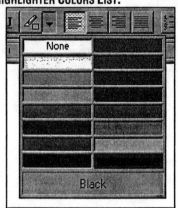

HYPHENATION

1. Click **Tools** menu .... `Alt`+`T`

2. Click **Hyphenation** .... `H`

The Hyphenation dialog box displays.

3. Choose from the following hyphenation options:

   - **A**utomatically Hyphenate Document........ `Alt`+`A`

   - Hyphenate Words in **C**APS..................... `Alt`+`C`

4. Click **Hyphenation Zone** scroll box............... `Alt`+`Z`

5. Type number .... *number*
   for hyphenation zone (default is **0.25"**).

6. Click **Limit Consecutive Hyphens To**............. `Alt`+`L`
   scroll box.

7. Type number .... *number*
   for maximum number of lines that can
   end in hyphens (default is **No Limit**).

continued...

To hyphenate a document manually:

a. Click **Manual...** .... `Alt`+`M`

The Manual Hyphenation dialog box displays.

b. Click mouse to change hyphen position.

c. Click **Yes** .... `Alt`+`Y`

to hyphenate word at selected position.

OR

Click **No** .... `Alt`+`N`

to skip current word and move to
next word to be hyphenated.

8. Click **OK** .... `↵`

LANGUAGE

Formats selected information in a different language, and selects the default language for the active template. Language formatting is used by the spelling and grammar tools, if the appropriate dictionary files are installed on your computer. (See SPELLING, page 203, and GRAMMAR, page 267, for more information. Also see your Word documentation for information obtaining additional language dictionaries.)

1. Select text you want to format in a different language.

2. Click **Tools** menu .... `Alt`+`T`

3. Click **Language** .... `L`

The Language dialog box displays.

4. Click **Mark Selected Text As** list box .... `Alt`+`M`

5. Click desired language .... `↑` `↓`

continued...

LANGUAGE (CONTINUED)

To change default language for active template:

a. Click `Default...` .... `Alt`+`D`

b. Click `Yes` .... `Alt`+`Y`
   when confirmation dialog box appears.

6. Click `OK` .... `↵`

PROTECT DOCUMENT

Word documents can be protected to allow reviewers to make comments on a document but not revisions by protecting it for annotations. Documents can also be protected to allow reviewers to make marked revisions only, which you can later review. In addition, documents can also be protected to only allow form fields to be filled. (See ANNOTATIONS, page 188, and FORMS, page 26, for more information. Also see SAVE OPTIONS, page 270, for information on assigning a password preventing a document from being opened.)

Protect Document Command

1. Click **Tools** menu .... `Alt`+`T`

2. Click **Protect Document** .... `P`

The Protect Document dialog box displays.

3. Choose one of the following **Protect Document For** option:

   • Revisions .... `Alt`+`R`

   • Annotations .... `Alt`+`A`

   • Forms .... `Alt`+`F`

   To protect specific sections of a form:

   a. Click `Sections...` .... `Alt`+`S`

   *NOTE: This option is only available if **Forms** was selected in step 3.*

continued...

PROTECT DOCUMENT COMMAND (CONTINUED)

The Section Protection dialog box displays.

b. Click **Protected Sections** list box............ `Alt` + `P`

c. Click sections....................... `↑` `↓` then `Space`
   you want to protect.

d. Click `OK` .... `↵`
   to close **Section Protection** dialog box.

The Protect Document dialog box redisplays.

To assign optional password to further protect document:

a. Click **Password** text box .... `Alt` + `P`

b. Type password .... *password*
   you want to use to protect document.

4. Click `OK` .... `↵`

Unprotect Document

1. Click **Tools** menu .... `Alt` + `T`

2. Click **Unprotect Document**.................................... `P`

   NOTE: If a password was selected with the
   Protect Document *command, above, the*
   Unprotect Document *dialog box displays,*
   prompting you for the selected password.

a. Type appropriate password .... *password*

b. Click `OK` .... `↵`

198

Protect Form Button

Toggles form protection for the active document, except for the filling in of form fields. (See PROTECT DOCUMENT COMMAND, pages 196 and 197, for information on password protecting a form, and for protecting specific sections of a form.)

Click **Protect Form** button...
on **Forms** toolbar.

REVISIONS

Revisions to a document by different reviewers can be noted with revision marks, which you can later accept or reject. How revision marks are displayed in a document is selected in the Revisions tab under Tools Options. (See REVISION OPTIONS, page 269, for more information.)

Turn Revisions On and Off

> *NOTE: When revision marks are turned on, the MRK message in the status bar is bold.*

1. Double-click **MRK** message .... MRK
    in status bar.

    OR

    a. Click **T**ools menu............................... Alt + T

    b. Click **Re**v**isions** V

    The Revisions dialog box displays.

2. Choose from the following **Document Revisions** options:

    •   **M**ark Revisions While Editing.................. Alt + M

    •   Show Revisions on **S**creen...................... Alt + S

    •   Show Revisions in **P**rinted Document ..... Alt + P

continued...

TURN REVISIONS ON AND OFF (CONTINUED)

To select how revision marks are displayed in document:

Click [Options...] .... `Alt`+`O`

(See REVISION OPTIONS, page 269, for more information.)

3. Click [OK] .... `↵`

Accept/Reject Revisions

Double-click **MRK** message .... `MRK`
in status bar.

OR

1. Click **Tools** menu .... `Alt`+`T`

2. Click **Revisions** .... `V`

The Revisions dialog box displays.

To accept all document revisions:

a. Click [Accept All] .... `Alt`+`A`

b. Click [Yes] .... `Alt`+`Y`
when confirmation dialog box appears.

To reject all document revisions:

a. Click [Reject All] .... `Alt`+`J`

b. Click [Yes] .... `Alt`+`Y`
when confirmation dialog box appears.

To review individual revisions:

a. Click [Review...] .... `Alt`+`R`

The Review Revisions dialog box displays.

continued...

200

b. Click **Find Next after Accept/Reject** .... 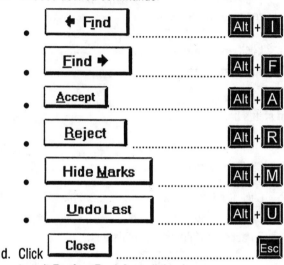 `Alt`+`N`
   check box to find next revision after
   selecting **Accept** or **Reject** buttons (if desired).

c. Choose desired commands:

   - **← Find** .... `Alt`+`I`

   - **Find →** .... `Alt`+`F`

   - **Accept** .... `Alt`+`A`

   - **Reject** .... `Alt`+`R`

   - **Hide Marks** .... `Alt`+`M`

   - **Undo Last** .... `Alt`+`U`

d. Click **Close** .... `Esc`
   to exit **Review Revisions** dialog box.

Compare Versions

Compares two versions of a document, inserting revision marks where a revised document differs from the original.

1. Double-click **MRK** message .... `MRK`
   in status bar.

   OR

   a. Click **Tools** menu .... `Alt`+`T`

   b. Click **Revisions** .... `V`

*The **Revisions** dialog box displays.*

2. Click **Compare Versions...** .... `Alt`+`C`

continued...

COMPARE VERSIONS (CONTINUED)

The Compare Versions dialog box displays. If the name of the file you want to compare appears in the Original File Name text box, proceed to step 8.

3. Click **List Files of Type** drop-down list box... `Alt`+`T`

4. Click file type you want to compare.................. `↑` `↓`

5. Click **Drives** drop-down list box.................... `Alt`+`V`

6. Type or Click drive letter .... *drive* or `↑` `↓`
   containing the file you want to compare.

7. Double-click directory in **Directories** list box containing file you want to compare.

   OR

   a. Click **Directories** list box .... `Alt`+`D`

   b. Click directory... `↑` `↓`

   c. Press **ENTER** .... `↵`

8. Double-click file in **Original File Name** list box.

   OR

   a. Click **Original File Name** list box .... `Alt`+`N`

   b. Type file name .... *file name*

   c. Click [**OK**] .... `↵`

NOTE: *If the revised document contains revision marks, a prompt displays, informing you Word may not be able to detect some of the existing revisions. Remove the revision marks with the procedures described in Accept/Reject Revisions, page 200.*

Merge Revisions

Merges revisions and annotations from an open, revised document into the original document.

1. Double-click **MRK** message .... `MRK`
   in status bar.

   OR

   a. Click **Tools** menu.. `Alt`+`T`

   b. Click **Revisions** .... `V`

*The **Revisions** dialog box displays.*

2. Click **Merge Revisions...** .... `Alt`+`E`

*The **Merge Revisions** dialog box displays. If the name of the file you want to merge appears in the **Original File Name** text box, proceed to step 8.*

3. Click **List Files of Type** drop-down list box .. `Alt`+`T`

4. Click file type you want to merge .... `↑` `↓`

5. Click **Drives** drop-down list box..................... `Alt`+`V`

6. Type or Click drive letter .... *drive* or `↑` `↓`
   containing file you want to merge.

7. Double-click directory in **Directories** list box containing
   file you want to merge.

   OR

   a. Click **Directories** list box .... `Alt`+`D`

   b. Click directory .... `↑` `↓`

   c. Press **ENTER** .... `↵`

8. Double-click file in **Original File Name** list box.

   OR

continued...

a. Click **Original File Name** list box .... Alt + N

b. Type file name .... *file name*

c. Click OK .... ↵

SPELLING

> *NOTE:* *Various spell checking options can be selected in the **Spelling** tab under **Tools Options**. (See **SPELLING OPTIONS**, page 271, for more information.)*

1. Place cursor in document where you want to begin spell check, or select text you want to spell check.

2. Click **Spelling** button .... ABC✓
   in **Standard** toolbar.

   OR

   a. Click **Tools** menu .... Alt + T

   b. Click **Spelling** .... S

   OR

   Press **F7** F7

*The **Spelling** dialog box displays. Word displays misspelled words in the **Not in Dictionary** text box. Suggested alternatives for the misspelled word are displayed in the **Suggestions** list box.*

   To choose alternative suggested word:

   a. Click **Suggestions** list box .... Alt + N

   b. Click word .... ↑ ↓

continued...

SPELLING (CONTINUED)

To select word not included in Suggestions list box:

a. Click **Change To** text box.................. `Alt`+`T`

b. Type replacement word ....*word*

3. Choose one of the following commands for each spelling error:

- **Ignore** .... `Alt`+`I`

  to ignore unrecognized word.

- **Ignore All** .... `Alt`+`G`

  to ignore all instances of unrecognized word.

- **Change** .... `Alt`+`C`

  to replace current instance of unrecognized word with selection in **Suggestions** box.

- **Change All** .... `Alt`+`L`

  to replace all instances of unrecognized word with selection in **Suggestions** box.

- **Add** .... `Alt`+`A`

  to add unrecognized word to dictionary.

To change dictionary to which you want to add unrecognized words:

a. Click **Add Words To** drop-down list box .. `Alt`+`W`

b. Click dictionary............................ `↑` `↓`

*(See **SPELLING OPTIONS**, page 271, for information on creating and editing custom dictionaries.)*

continued...

- **S̲uggest** **Alt** + **S**

  to suggest replacement words
  from main dictionary and open custom dictionaries.

- **AutoCo̲rrect** **Alt** + **R**

  to add unrecognized word to **AutoCorrect**
  list. *(See **AUTOCORRECT**, page 190, for more
  information.)*

- **O̲ptions...** **Alt** + **O**

  to access **Spelling** tab under **Tools Options**.
  *(See **SPELLING OPTIONS**, page 271, for more
  information.)*

- **U̲ndo Last** **Alt** + **U**

  to reverse last action.

4. **Cancel** **Esc**

   to exit **Spelling** dialog box
   without making any changes.

   OR

   Close **Esc**

   to exit **Spelling** dialog box
   after making desired changes.

Automatic Spell Checking

Marks unrecognized words in a document with a red wavy line.

1. Activate automatic spell checking following procedures
   under **Spelling Options**, page 271.

2. Correct marked words by pointing at Word with mouse
   and clicking left mouse button.

A Shortcut Menu displays.

continued...

AUTOMATIC SPELL CHECKING (CONTINUED)

3. Click correct spelling suggestion in **Shortcut Menu** or select from the following options:

- Ignore All .... ⬆️⬇️
  to ignore all instances of the word.

- Add .... ⬆️⬇️
  to add the word to your custom dictionary.

- Spelling.. ⬆️⬇️
  to spell check the entire document.

THESAURUS

1. Select word or phrase for which you want to find a synonym, antonym, or related word.

2. a. Click **Tools** menu.................................. Alt + T

   b. Click **Thesaurus** .... T

   OR

   Press **Shift+F7**.. Shift + F7

   NOTE: *The **Thesaurus** dialog box displays. The selected word or phrase appears in the **Looked Up** drop-down list box. If the selected word or phrase is not found, an alphabetical list displays with possible alternatives.*

   To look up definition for word displayed in Looked Up drop-down list box:

   a. Click **Meanings** list box........................ Alt + M

   b. Click meaning.. ⬆️⬇️

   c. Click [**Look Up**] .... Alt + L

continued...

To look up synonym for word or phrase displayed in Looked Up drop-down list box:

a. Click **Replace with Synonym** list box ...... `Alt`+`S`

b. Click synonym .... `↑` `↓`

c. Click [**Look Up**] .... `Alt`+`L`

To select different word looked up during the current thesaurus session:

a. Click **Looked Up** drop-down list box .... `Alt`+`K`

b. Click word or phrase .... `↑` `↓`

   OR

   Click [**Previous**] .... `Alt`+`P`

3. Click [**Replace**] .... `Alt`+`R`
   to replace word or phrase in document with selection
   in **Replace with Synonym** text box.

WORD COUNT

1. Click **Tools** menu .... `Alt`+`T`

2. Click **Word Count** .... `W`

*The **Word Count** dialog box displays with counted statistics for the active document.*

3. Click **Include Footnotes and Endnotes** .... `Alt`+`F`
   to include footnotes and endnotes when
   compiling document statistics.

4. Click [**Close**] .... `Esc`
   to exit **Word Count** dialog box.

208

MAIL OPTIONS
ADDRESS BOOK

Inserts names and address from address books created with Microsoft Exchange Server, Schedule+ 2.0 contact lists, or other MAPI-compatible messaging system address lists.

> *NOTE: This option is also available in several dialog boxes and wizards.*

1. Place cursor in document where you want to insert entries from your address book.

2. Click **Insert Address** button .... 📖 ▼

The Select Name dialog displays.

3. Click **Show Names from the** .... `Alt`+`S`
   drop-down list box.

4. Click desired address list .... `↑` `↓`

5. Click **Type Name or Select From List** .... `Alt`+`Y`
   text box.

6. Click desired name... `↑` `↓`

   To create a new address book:

   Click `New...` .... `Alt`+`N`

   To display properties for the selected address book:

   Click `Properties` .... `Alt`+`R`

7. Click `OK` .... `↵`

   > *NOTE: You can also select from a list of recently used address by clicking the drop-down arrow next to the **Address** button.*

ENVELOPES AND LABELS

Create Envelope

1. Select delivery address contained in current document. If current document does not contain address you want to print, leave cursor as flashing insertion point.

2. Click **Tools** menu .... `Alt`+`T`

3. Click **Envelopes and Labels** .... `E`

The Envelopes and Labels dialog box displays.

4. Click **Envelopes** tab .... `Alt`+`E`

5. Click **Delivery Address** list box .... `Alt`+`D`

6. Type delivery address ....*address*
    or make any desired edits
    to address selected in step **1**.

    > *NOTE:* By default, Word uses the mailing address
    > in the **User Info** tab of the **Options** dialog
    > box as the return address. (See **USER
    > INFO**, page 274, for more information.)

    To select an address from your Address Book:

    a. Click **Insert Address** button .... 📖▾

    b. Follow procedures 2 through 7 under **Address Book**,
        page 208.

    OR

    1. Click drop-down arrow next to **Address** button.

    A list of most recently used address displays.

    2. Click desired address.

    To select different return address:

    a. Click **Return Address** list box .... `Alt`+`R`

    b. Type return address....................................*address*
        or make desired changes to default address.

continued...

CREATE ENVELOPE (CONTINUED)

To omit return address from envelope:

Click **Om**it check box .... `Alt` + `M`

7. Click | **Print** | .... `Alt` + `P`

OR

Click | **Add to Document** | .... `Alt` + `A`

*NOTE: If you made any changes to the return
address, a prompt displays, asking if you
want to save the new return address as the
default.*

ENVELOPE OPTIONS

1. Click **Tools** menu .... `Alt` + `T`

2. Click **Envelopes and Labels** .... `E`

The Envelopes and Labels dialog box displays.

3. Click **Envelopes** tab .... `Alt` + `E`

4. Click | **Options...** | .... `Alt` + `O`

The Envelope Options dialog box displays.

5. Click **Envelope Options** tab......................... `Alt` + `E`

6. Click **Envelope Size** drop-down list box .... `Alt` + `S`

7. Click envelope size... `↑` `↓`

8. Choose desired **If Mailed in the USA** options:

• Delivery Point **B**ar Code .... `Alt` + `B`

• FIM-**A** Courtesy Reply Mail...................... `Alt` + `A`

*NOTE: This option is only available if **Delivery
Point Bar Code** is selected.*

continued...

CREATE ENVELOPE (CONTINUED)

To change fonts for delivery and return addresses:

a. Click [**F**ont...] .... `Alt`+`F`
to change delivery address font.

OR

Click [**F**o**nt**...] .... `Alt`+`O`
to change return address font.

The Envelope Address or Envelope Return Address dialog box displays.

b. Follow procedures under **FORMAT FONT COMMAND**, page 78.

To change delivery address placement:

a. Click **From Left** scroll box..................... `Alt`+`L`

OR

Click **From Top** scroll box..................... `Alt`+`T`

b. Type number .... *number*
for distance from edge of page (default is **Auto**).

To change return address placement:

a. Click **From Left** scroll box..................... `Alt`+`M`

OR

Click **From Top** scroll box..................... `Alt`+`R`

b. Type number .... *number*
for distance from edge of page (default is **Auto**).

9. Click [**OK**] .... `⏎`

PRINTING OPTIONS

1. Click **Tools** menu .... `Alt`+`T`

2. Click **Envelopes and Labels** .... `E`

continued...

CREATE ENVELOPE (CONTINUED)

The Envelopes and Labels dialog box displays.

3. Click **E**nvelopes tab .... `Alt`+`E`

4. Click [**O**ptions...] .... `Alt`+`O`

The Envelope Options dialog box displays.

5. Click **P**rinting Options tab .... `Alt`+`P`

6. Choose desired **Feed Method** options:

   • Face **U**p .... `Alt`+`U`

   • Face **D**own .... `Alt`+`D`

   • Clockwise **R**otation.......................... `Alt`+`C`

7. Click desired feed method .... `Tab` then `←` `→`
   displayed in Feed Method option group.

8. Click **F**eed From drop-down list box............ `Alt`+`F`

9. Click printer tray .... `↑` `↓`
   to use to feed envelopes into printer.

   To return Printing Options tab to settings proposed by Word:

   Click [**R**eset] .... `Alt`+`R`

10. Click [**OK**] .... `↵`

Create Labels

1. Select address contained in current document. If current document does not contain address you want to print, leave cursor as flashing insertion point.

2. Click **T**ools menu.................................. `Alt`+`T`

3. Click **E**nvelopes and Labels .... `E`

continued...

The Envelopes and Labels dialog box displays.

4. Click **L**abels tab .... `Alt`+`L`

5. Click **A**ddress list box............................ `Alt`+`A`

6. Type address .... *address*
   or make any edits to address selected in step 1.

   To use name and address stored in User Info tab of Options dialog box *(See USER INFO, page 274, for more information)*:

   Click **Use Return Address**............................ `Alt`+`R`

   To select an address from your Address Book:

   a. Click **Insert Address** button .... `📖▼`

   b. Follow procedures 2 through 7 under **Address Book**, page 208.

   OR

   1. Click drop-down arrow next to **Address** button.

   A list of most recently used address displays.

   2. Click desired address.

7. Click **Delivery Point Bar Code** .... `Alt`+`B`
   to print POSTNET (Postal Numeric Encloding Technique) bar code.

8. Click **Full Page of the Same Label** .... `Alt`+`F`
   OR

   a. Click **Single Label** .... `Alt`+`N`

   b. Click **Row** .... `Alt`+`W`
      OR

      Click **Column** .... `Alt`+`C`

continued...

CREATE LABELS (CONTINUED)

    c. Type number .... *number*
       of rows or columns.

9. Click **Print** .... `Alt`+`P`

    OR

    Click **New Document** .... `Alt`+`D`

    NOTE: *This option is unavailable if **Single Label**
               was selected in previous step.*

LABEL OPTIONS

1. Click **Tools** menu .... `Alt`+`T`

2. Click **Envelopes and Labels** .... `E`

The Envelopes and Labels dialog box displays.

3. Click **Labels** tab .... `Alt`+`L`

4. Click **Options...** .... `Alt`+`O`

The Label Options dialog box displays.

5. Click **Dot Matrix** .... `Alt`+`M`

    OR

    a. Click **Laser** .... `Alt`+`L`

    b. Click **Tray** drop-down list box.................. `Alt`+`T`

    c. Click printer tray .... `↑` `↓`

6. Click **Label Products** drop-down list box...... `Alt`+`P`

7. Click label type... `↑` `↓`

8. Click **Product Numbers** list box .... `Alt`+`N`

9. Click label product number.............................. `↑` `↓`

continued...

CREATE LABELS (CONTINUED)

To change the margin size, label size, and distance between labels:

a. Click [**Details...**] .... [Alt]+[D]

The Custom Label Information dialog box displays. The title of the dialog box changes to reflect the selected type of label.

NOTE: *Various options in the **Custom Label Information** dialog box are not available for all label types.*

b. Choose dimensions to change from the following options:

- Top Margin .... [Alt]+[T]

- Size Margin .... [Alt]+[S]

- Vertical Pitch .... [Alt]+[V]

- Horizontal Pitch .... [Alt]+[O]

- Label Height .... [Alt]+[E]

- Label Width .... [Alt]+[W]

- Number Across .... [Alt]+[A]

- Number Down .... [Alt]+[D]

c. Type number .... *number* for new dimension.

10. Click [**OK**] .... [↵]

MAIL MERGE

*A mail merge combines the contents of two documents: a **main
document** and a **data source**. A main document contains information
that does not change, such as the body of a letter. Main documents
can include form letters, labels, and envelopes. A data source contains
information, known as **records**, that vary with each merged document.*

*Creating a mail merge involves several steps: creating the main
document; creating the data source; inserting merge fields into the
main document; then merging the two completed documents together.
Word contains a feature, the **Mail Merge Helper**, to assist in this
process.*

*The following procedures describe how to set up a basic mail merge.
(See your Word documentation, or refer to on-line **Help** for
information on advanced options and techniques.)*

Set Up Main Document

> *NOTE:* *This command is also used to restore a
> mail merge main document to a normal
> Word document.*

1. Open document you want to use for the mail merge
   main document. If you are creating a new main
   document, skip to step 2.

2. Click **Tools** menu .... Alt + T

3. Click **Mail Merge** .... R

The Mail Merge Helper dialog box displays.

4. Click [**Create** ▼] .... Alt + C

5. Choose main document type from the following options:

   - Form **L**etters L

   - **M**ailing Labels .... M

   - **E**nvelopes .... E

   - **C**atalog C

   - Restore to **N**ormal Word Document .... N

continued...

SET UP MAIN DOCUMENT (CONTINUED)

NOTE: *This option is only available if the active
document is a mail merge main document.*

*A prompt displays, asking if you want to use the active window or
create a new document to use as the mail merge main document.*

6. Click | **Active Window** | .... Alt + A

   OR

   Click | **New Main Document** | .... Alt + N

The Mail Merge Helper dialog box redisplays.

7. Click | **Close** | .... Esc

   to return to mail merge main document.

   OR

   Follow procedures under **Attach Data Source**, below.

Mail Merge Toolbar

*After creating a mail merge main document, the Mail Merge toolbar
displays. The Mail Merge toolbar buttons and their associated
commands are as follows:*

| Insert Merge Field | *Inserts a merge field into the document at the location of the cursor.* |

| Insert Word Field | *Inserts a Word field into the document at the location of the cursor.* |

 *View Merged Data button. Toggles
between displaying merge fields and
records from the data source.*

 *First Record button. Displays how the
first record in the attached data source
appears when merged with the main
document.*

continued...

218

MAIL MERGE TOOLBAR (CONTINUED)

 Previous Record button. Displays how the previous record in the attached data source appears when merged with the main document.

 Go To Record box. Selects a specific record to display from attached data source when merged with the main document.

 Next Record button. Displays how the next record in the attached data source appears when merged with the main document.

 Last Record button. Displays how the last record in the attached data source appears when merged with the main document.

 Mail Merge Helper button. Displays the **Mail Merge Helper** dialog box.

 Check for Errors button. Checks the mail merge for errors.

 Merge to New Document button. Automatically merges the main document and the data source to a new document.

 Merge to Printer button. Automatically merges the main document and the data source to a printer.

 Mail Merge button. Displays the **Merge** dialog box, used for selecting specific records to merge, query options, and other choices when merging the main document and data source.

 Find Record button. Searches for a specific record in the attached mail merge data source.

Edit Data Source button. Displays the **Data Form** dialog box, used for managing records in the data source.

Attach Data Source

Creates a new data source or opens an existing data source. This command also allows you to specify a separate header row file for the data source. A header row is the top row in a data source table containing merge fields which identify the various types of information contained in the data source.

CREATE DATA SOURCE

1. Follow procedures under **Set Up Main Document**, page 216.

2. Click **Tools** menu .... Alt + T

3. Click **Mail Merge** .... R

   The Mail Merge Helper dialog box displays.

4. Click | **Get Data ▼** | .... Alt + G

   NOTE: This option is unavailable if active Word document has not been set up as a mail merge main document.

5. **Create Data Source** C

   The Create Data Source dialog box displays.

   NOTE: Commonly used field names are listed in the **Field Names in Header Row** list box.

   To add field names:

   a. Click **Field Name** text box .... Alt + F

   b. Type field name .... *field name*

   c. Click | **Add Field Name ▶▶** | .... Alt + A

   To remove field names:

   a. Click **Field Names in Header Row** .... Alt + N
      list box

continued.

ATTACH DATA SOURCE (CONTINUED)

b. Click field name .... ⬆ ⬇
you want to remove.

c. Click | **Remove Field Name** | .... `Alt` + `R`

To reorder field names:

a. Click **Field Names in Header Row** .... `Alt` + `N`
list box.

b. Click field name .... ⬆ ⬇
you want to move.

c. Click **Up Arrrow** or **Down Arrow** buttons . ⬆ ⬇

6. Click | **OK** | .... ⏎

The Save Data Source dialog box displays.

7. Follow procedures under **SAVE FILE**, page 43.

After saving the data source file, a prompt displays, asking if you want to edit the data source or the main document.

8. Click | **Edit Data Source** | .... `Alt` + `D`

The Data Form dialog box displays.

> NOTE: *The field names selected in step 5 appear in the **Field Names** list box.*

To add new records:

a. Click left mouse button to move between field name
text boxes in **Field Name** list box.

OR

Press **Tab** or **Shift+Tab** .... `Tab` or `Shift` + `Tab`

b. Type information ....*text*
into selected field name text boxes.

continued...

c. Click | **Add New** | .... `Alt`+`A`

d. Repeat steps a through c to add additional records.

To move between records:

Click one of the following buttons:

- Next Record .... `▶`

- Previous Record.. `◀`

- First Record... `◀◀`

- Last Record... `▶▶`

OR

a. Click **Record** text box............................... `Alt`+`R`

b. Type record number .... *number*

c. Press **ENTER** .... `↵`

9. Choose one of the following options.

- | **Delete** | .... `Alt`+`D`
  to remove selected record from data source.

- | **Restore** | .... `Alt`+`S`
  to restore selected record to its
  original contents.

- | **Find...** | .... `Alt`+`F`
  to search data source for specified
  information.

- | **View Source** | .... `Alt`+`V`
  to view data source file in table form.

continued...

ATTACH DATA SOURCE (CONTINUED)

> *NOTE: Viewing the data source file allows you to edit data records using the **Database** toolbar.*

10. Click `OK` .... ⏎

OPEN DATA SOURCE

1. Follow procedures under **Set Up Main Document**, page 216.

2. Click **T**ools menu .... Alt + T

3. Click **Mail Merge** .... R

The Mail Merge Helper dialog box displays.

4. Click `Get Data ▼` .... Alt + G

> *NOTE: This option is unavailable if active Word document has not been set up as a mail merge main document.*

5. Click **O**pen Data Source .... O

6. Follow procedures under **OPEN FILE**, page 35.

USE ADDRESS BOOK

1. Follow procedures under **Set Up Main Document**, page 216.

2. Click **T**ools menu .... Alt + T

3. Click **Mail Merge** .... R

The Mail Merge Helper dialog box displays.

4. Click `Get Data ▼` .... Alt + G

> *NOTE: This option is unavailable if active Word document has not been set up as a mail merge main document.*

continued...

5. Click **Use Address Book**.................................... [A]

The Use Address Book dialog box displays.

6. Click desired address book .... [A]
    from **Choose Address Book** list box.

Address books display that were created with Microsoft Exchange Server, Schedule+ 2.0 contact lists, or other MAPI-compatible messaging system address lists.

7. Click [OK] .... [↵]

HEADER OPTIONS

1. Follow procedures under **Set Up Main Document**, page 216.

2. Click **Tools** menu .... [Alt]+[T]

3. Click **Mail Merge** .... [R]

The Mail Merge Helper dialog box displays.

4. Click [**Get Data** ▼] .... [Alt]+[G]

    NOTE: *This option is unavailable if active Word document has not been set up as a mail merge main document.*

5. Click **Header Options**................................. [H]

A prompt displays, asking if you want to create a new header file or open an existing header file.

6. Click [**Create...**] .... [Alt]+[C]

    OR

    Click [**Open...**] .... [Alt]+[O]

continued...

224

ATTACH DATA SOURCE (CONTINUED)

*NOTES: If you selected **Create** in step 6, the **Create Header Source** dialog box displays. Commonly used field names are listed in the **Field Names in Header Row** list box.*

*If you selected **Open**, follow the procedures for opening a file under **OPEN FILE**, page 35, then skip to step 9.*

To add field names:

a. Click **F̲ield Name** text box .... `Alt` + `F`

b. Type field name .... *field name*

c. Click `A̲dd Field Name ▶▶` .... `Alt` + `A`

To remove field names:

a. Click **Field N̲ames in Header Row** .... `Alt` + `N`
list box

b. Click field name .... `↑` `↓`
you want to remove.

c. Click `R̲emove Field Name` .... `Alt` + `R`

To reorder field names:

a. Click **Field N̲ames in Header Row** .... `Alt` + `N`
list box.

b. Click field name .... `↑` `↓`
you want to move.

c. Click **Up Arrrow** or .... `↑` or `↓`
Down Arrow buttons

7. Click `OK` .... `↵`

The Save Header Source dialog box displays.

continued...

8. Follow procedures under **SAVE FILE**, page 43.

After saving the header source file, the Mail Merge Helper dialog box redisplays.

9. Follow procedures under **Create Data Source** or **Open Data Source**, above.

Insert Merge Fields into Main Document

INSERT MERGE FIELD DIALOG BOX

1. Place cursor in mail merge main document where you want to insert merge field.

2. Press **Shift+Alt+F** .... `Shift` + `Alt` + `F`

The Insert Merge Field dialog box displays.

3. Click **Mail Merge Fields** list box .... `Alt` + `M`

4. Click desired merge field .... `↑` `↓`

5. Click **Word Fields** list box .... `Alt` + `W`

6. Click desired Word field .... `↑` `↓`

7. Repeat steps 1 through 6 to insert additional merge fields.

8. Click `OK` .... `↵`

TOOLBAR

1. Place cursor in mail merge main document where you want to insert merge field.

2. Click **Insert Merge Field** button .... `Insert Merge Field`
   in **Mail Merge** toolbar.

continued...

INSERT MERGE FIELDS INTO MAIN DOCUMENT (CONTINUED)

3. Click desired merge field.

    To insert a Word field:

    a. Click **Insert Word Field** button .... | Insert Word Field |
        in **Mail Merge** toolbar.

    b. Click desired Word field.

4. Repeat steps 1 through 3 to insert additional merge
    fields.

Merge Main Document and Data Source

*Merges the main document and attached data source with the **Tools
Mail Merge** command. This command contains allows you to select
query options and various other choices.*

1. Click **Mail Merge** button ....
    in **Mail Merge** toolbar.

    OR

    a. Click **Tools** menu .... `Alt`+`T`

    b. Click **Mail Merge** .... `R`

*The **Mail Merge Helper** dialog box displays.*

    c. Click | **Merge...** | .... `Alt`+`M`

*The **Merge** dialog box displays.*

2. Click **Merge To** drop-down list box .... `Alt`+`R`

3. Choose one of the following options:

    • New Document .... `↑` `↓`

    • Printer .... `↑` `↓`

4. Click **All** .... `Alt`+`A`
    to merge all records in data source.

    OR

continued...

MERGE MAIN DOCUMENT & DATA SOURCE (CONTINUED)

a. Click **From** text box .... `Alt`+`F`

b. Type number .... *number*
   of first record in range or records to merge.

c. Click **To** text box .... `Alt`+`T`

d. Type number .... *number*
   of last record in range or records to merge.

5. Choose one of the following **When Merging Records**
   options:

   - **D**on't print blank lines when .... `Alt`+`D`
     data fields are empty

   - **P**rint blank lines when .... `Alt`+`P`
     data fields are empty

6. Click [**Check Errors...**] .... `Alt`+`E`

The Checking and Reporting Errors dialog box displays.

7. Click error checking option:

   - **S**imulate the merge and report .... `Alt`+`S`
     errors in a new document

   - **C**omplete the merge, pausing to .... `Alt`+`C`
     report each error as it occurs

   - Complete the **m**erge without pausing ...... `Alt`+`M`
     Report errors in a new document

8. Click [**OK**] .... `↵`

The Merge dialog box redisplays.

   To select query options for mail merge:

   Click [**Query Options...**] .... `Alt`+`Q`

9. Click [**Merge...**] .... `↵`

Keyboard

Selects various mail merge commands using keyboard shortcuts. After creating the main document and data source using the above procedures, select any of the following keystrokes:

Command	Press
Preview mail merge	**Shift** + **Alt** + **K**
Merge document......................................	**Shift** + **Alt** + **N**
Print merged document...........................	**Shift** + **Alt** + **M**
Edit mail merge....................................... data document	**Shift** + **Alt** + **E**
Insert merge field...................................	**Shift** + **Alt** + **F**

COMPOUND DOCUMENTS

A *compound document* refers to a document that has been created with information from more than one application. For example, a compound document can contain data from graphic, spreadsheet, and database programs.

Information created from other applications can be imported directly using the *Copy* and *Paste* commands. Imported information can also be **linked** to its source, or **embedded** directly into a Word document as an **object** entirely self-contained and not linked to any external files or applications. Links and embedded objects in a document are created using fields. (See FIELDS, page 88, for more information.)

DRAWING TOOLS

Word's Drawing toolbar contains a variety of tools for creating and editing graphics in a Word document. Symbols, text boxes, and other graphic items can be drawn directly onto a page while in Print Preview or Page Layout View, or a Word 6.0 Picture object can be created in a separate window and embedded in a document. Word's drawing tools can also be used to modify imported graphics, such as clipart files.

Create/Edit Graphic Items

NOTE: *Graphic items can only be created and edited from **Print Preview** or **Page Layout View**.*

1.   Click **Drawing** button ....
     in **Standard** toolbar.

The screen display switches to Page Layout View and the Drawing toolbar displays.

2.   Create and edit graphic items using tools from **Drawing** toolbar.

230

Word Picture

*Creates and edits **Word Picture** objects and edits imported graphics.*

CREATE PICTURE

Creates a new Microsoft Word Picture object.

1. Place cursor in document where you want to create a new picture.

2. Click **Create Picture** button .... in **Drawing** toolbar.

   OR

   a. Click **Insert** menu .... `Alt`+`I`

   b. Click **Object** .... `O`

   c. Click **Create New** tab .... `Alt`+`C`

   d. Click **Microsoft Word Picture** .... `↑` `↓` from **Object Type** list box.

   e. Click `OK` .... `↵`

*A picture window displays, along with the **Picture** toolbar.*

3. Create and edit graphic items using tools from **Drawing** toolbar.

   To adjust picture boundaries to fit graphic items:

   Click **Reset Picture Boundary** button .... in **Picture** toolbar.

   To close picture and return to document:

   Click `Close Picture` .... `Shift`+`Alt`+`C` from **Picture** toolbar.

EDIT PICTURE

> NOTE: An imported graphic modified with this command is converted to a **Word Picture** object. Any links with external files are broken.

1. Double-click **Word Picture** object or imported graphic you want to edit.

   OR

   a. Click object or graphic.

   b. Click **Edit** menu.. Alt + E

   c. Click **Picture** I

A picture window displays, along with the Picture toolbar.

2. Create and edit graphic items using tools from **Drawing** toolbar.

   To adjust picture boundaries to fit graphic items:

   Click **Reset Picture Boundary** button..................
   in **Picture** toolbar.

   To close picture and return to document:

   Click ⬚ Close Picture .... Shift + Alt + C
   from **Picture** toolbar.

EDIT LINKS

Displays, changes, and updates links in a document.

1. Click **Edit** menu.. Alt + E

2. Click **Links** .... K

   > NOTE: The **Edit Links** command is unavailable if the document does not contain any links.

The Links dialog box displays.

continued...

232

3. Click **Source File** list box............................. `Alt`+`S`

The Source File list box displays the source file, item, link type, and selected update option.

4. Click source file .... `↑` `↓`
    you want to change or update.

    NOTE: Select multiple fields by holding down
    Shift *with above procedures. Select multiple, non-contiguous fields by holding down* ***Ctrl*** *and clicking with the mouse.*

5. Choose one of the following update options:

    - **A**utomatic... `Alt`+`A`

    - **M**anual... `Alt`+`M`

    To prevent link from being updated:

    Click **Loc**k**ed** check box .... `Alt`+`K`

6. Click **Save Picture in Document**................... `Alt`+`S`
    to store a graphic a the Word document
    along with its link.

    NOTES: Selecting the ***Save Picture In Document*** *check box increases the size of the Word file since a complete representation of the graphic is stored in the document. Deselect this check box to decrease the size of the Word file.*

7. Choose from the following commands:

    - **Update Now** .... `Alt`+`U`
      to immediately update all source files
      selected in step 4.

continued...

*NOTES: This option is unavailable if **Locked** check
box was selected in step 5.*

*You can also update a link by selecting it in
the document and pressing F9.*

- .... **Alt** + **O**

  to open selected source file in its
  originating application

*NOTE: This option is unavailable if multiple source
files were selected in step 4.*

- .... **Alt** + **N**

  to change selected source files selected in step 4.

- .... **Alt** + **B**

  breaks link with source for all files
  selected in step 4.

8. Click .... ⏎

EMBEDDED OBJECTS

*An embedded object is information created in another application, yet
entirely self-contained within a Word document. Although not linked
to any external files, embedded objects can be edited and updated in
their source applications from within Word. In addition to the
following procedures, embedded objects can also be created with the
Paste Special command. (See PASTE SPECIAL, page 250, for more
information).*

Create New

1. Click **Insert** menu .... **Alt** + **I**

2. Click **Object** .... **O**

The Object dialog box displays.

continued...

234

3. Click **Create New** tab .... `Alt`+`C`

4. Click **Object Type** list box .... `Alt`+`O`

5. Click application.. `↑` `↓`
   from which to create object.

   NOTE: *Choices vary depending on applications*
   available to your computer.

6. Click **Display as Icon** check box .... `Alt`+`A`
   to display object as icon in document.

   To change icon representing embedded object:

   a. Click [**Change Icon...**] .... `Alt`+`I`

   NOTE: *This option is only available if **Display as***
   ***Icon** check box has been selected.*

   *The **Change Icon** dialog box displays.*

   b. Click **Icon** list box .... `Alt`+`I`

   c. Click icon.. `↑` `↓`

   The name of the file that contains the available icons appears at the
   bottom of the dialog box.

   To search for other files that contain icons:

   Click [**Browse...**] .... `Alt`+`B`

   d. Click **Caption** text box .... `Alt`+`C`
      to change caption for selected icon.

   e. Type caption...*text*

   d. Click [**OK**] .... `↵`
      to close **Change Icon** dialog box.

continued...

7. Click [**OK**] .... [←]
    to create object.

The selected application opens.

8. Create desired information.

9. Click **File** menu .... [Alt]+[F]
    from within the application.

10. Click **Update** .... [U]

11. a. Click **File** menu .... [Alt]+[F]
        from within the application.

    b. Click **Exit** .... [X]

    OR

    Press **Alt+F4** .... [Alt]+[F4]

    *NOTE: Ways of saving and exiting vary with
            different applications. Steps 9 through 11
            are generic procedures for saving and
            exiting in many applications, but not all.
            For more information, see the
            documentation for the applications you are
            using.*

Create from File

Inserts an embedded object based on an existing file.

1. Click **Insert** menu .... [Alt]+[I]

2. Click **Object** .... [O]
    *NOTE: The **Object** dialog box displays.*

3. Click **Create from File** tab .... [Alt]+[F]

4. Click **File Name** text box .... [Alt]+[N]

continued...

236

CREATE FROM FILE (CONTINUED)

5. Type file name .... *file name*
   OR

   a. Click [Browse...] ..... `Alt` + `B`

The Browse dialog box displays.

   b. Follow procedures under **OPEN FILE**, page 35.

6. Click **Link to File** check box........................... `Alt` + `K`
   to link selected file to its source.

7. Click **Display as Icon** check box .... `Alt` + `A`
   to display object as icon in document.

   To change icon representing object:

   a. Click [**Change Icon...**] .... `Alt` + `I`

   NOTE: *This option is only available if **Display as***
            ***Icon** check box has been selected.*

The Change Icon dialog box displays.

   b. Click **Icon** list box .... `Alt` + `I`

   c. Click icon... `↑` `↓`

The name of the file containing available icons appears at the bottom
of the dialog box.

   To search for other files that contain icons:

   Click [**Browse...**] .... `Alt` + `B`

   d. Click **Caption** text box .... `Alt` + `C`
      to change caption for selected icon.

   e. Type caption...*text*

   f. Click [**OK**] .... `↵`
      to close **Change Icon** dialog box.

8. Click [**OK**] .... `↵`

Edit Object

1. Double-click object you want to edit.

   OR

   a. Click object you want to edit.

   b. Click **E**dit menu... `Alt`+`E`

   c. Click **O**bject .... `O`

   NOTES: This option is unavailable if an object was not selected in step b.

   *The name of the **Object** command changes depending on the selected object (e.g., **Excel Worksheet Object, Paintbrush Picture Object**, etc.).*

   d. Click **E**dit .... `E`

   NOTE: The selected object opens in its originating application.

2. Make desired edits

3. Click **F**ile menu.. `Alt`+`F`
   from within the application.

4. Click **U**pdate .... `U`

5. a. Click **F**ile menu.. `Alt`+`F`
   from within the application.

   b. Click E**x**it... `X`

   OR

   Press **Alt+F4** .... `Alt`+`F4`

   NOTE: Ways of saving and exiting vary with different applications. Steps 3 through 5 are generic procedures for saving and exiting in many applications, but not all. For more information, see the documentation for the applications you are using.

Convert

Changes the source application for a selected embedded object.

1. Click object whose source application you want to change.

2. Click **Edit** menu...

3. Click **Object** ....

   NOTES: *This option is unavailable if an object was not selected in step 1.*

   *The name of the **Object** command changes depending on the selected object (e.g., **Edit Excel Worksheet Object** or **Paintbrush Picture Object Edit**).*

4. Click **Convert** ....

   The Convert dialog box displays.

   *The source application for the selected object displays next to **Convert Type** at the top of the dialog box.*

5. Click **Object Type** list box ....

   NOTE: *The **Object Type** list box displays the applications installed on your computer that are compatible with the selected object. If the only available application is the source application displayed next to **Convert Type** at the top of the dialog box, then there are no other applications installed on your computer capable of reading the selected object.*

6. Click application...
   to which you want to convert selected object.

continued...

7. Click **Convert To**................................... `Alt`+`C`
   to permanently convert object
   to application selected in step 6.

   OR

   Click **Activate As**................................... `Alt`+`A`
   to temporarily convert object
   to application selected in step 6.

8. Click **Display as Icon** check box .... `Alt`+`D`
   to display object as icon in document.
   To change icon representing object:

   a. Click `Change Icon...` .... `Alt`+`I`

   NOTE: *This option is only available if **Display as***
   ***Icon** check box has been selected.*
   The Change Icon dialog box displays.

   b. Click **Icon** list box .... `Alt`+`I`

   c. Click icon................................. `↑``↓`

   The name of the file containing available icons appears at the bottom
   of the dialog box.

   To search for other files containing icons:

   Click `Browse...` .... `Alt`+`B`

   d. Click **Caption** text box...................... `Alt`+`C`
      to change caption for selected icon.

   e. Type caption .... *text*

   f. Click `OK` .... `↵`
      to close **Change Icon** dialog box.

9. Click `OK` .... `↵`
   to convert object.

FORMAT PICTURE

*Graphics imported into a document or created using Word's drawing tools can resized, scaled, or cropped using the **Format Picture** command or the mouse.*

The height and width of a graphic can be resized independently of each other or simultaneously. A graphic can also be scaled so its dimensions are in proportion to its original size.

Cropping is used to trim unneeded portions of a graphic or to increase or decrease the amount of white space surrounding a graphic.

Format Picture Command

*Sizes, scales, and crops graphics using the **Format Picture** command.*

1.   Click graphic whose size, scaling, or cropping you want to change.

2.   Click **Format** menu .... `Alt`+`O`

3.   Click **Picture** .... `R`

   NOTES: This option is unavailable if a graphic was not selected in step 1.

*The **Picture** dialog box displays. The original dimensions of the selected graphic are displayed in the **Original Size** box.*

4.   a. Choose from the following **Crop From** options:

   • L̲eft .... `Alt`+`L`

   • R̲ight... `Alt`+`R`

   • T̲op .... `Alt`+`O`

   • B̲ottom... `Alt`+`B`

   b. Type number .... *number*
       for crop dimension.

continued...

FORMAT PICTURE COMMAND (CONTINUED)

5. a. Choose from the following **Scaling** options:

- Width.. Alt + W

- Height.. Alt + E

b. Type scaling percentage .... *number*

NOTE: *Any changes to **Scaling** options are also reflected in **Size** options, below.*

6. a. Choose from the following **Size** options:

- Width.. Alt + I

- Height.. Alt + T

b. Type size.. *number*

NOTE: *Any changes to **Size** options are also reflected in **Scaling** options, above.*

To remove cropping and return graphic to its original size:

Click [Reset] .... Alt + S

To format frame for selected graphic:

Click [Frame...] .... Alt + F

NOTE: *The **Frame** button is only available if a frame has been added to the selected graphic. (See **FRAMES**, page 93, for more information.)*

7. Click [OK] .... ⏎

Mouse

SIZE AND SCALE

1. Click graphic whose size and scaling you want to change.

Sizing handles appear on the top, bottom, right, and left edges, and in each corner of the selected graphic. The sizing handles in the corners resize the graphic proportionally, while the sizing handles on the top, bottom, left, and right edges resize the graphic vertically and horizontally.

2. Move mouse on top of sizing handle until pointer changes to a double-headed arrow.
3. Hold left mouse button.
4. Drag to desired size.
5. Release mouse button.

The scaling dimensions display as percentages in the status bar.

CROP

1. Click graphic whose cropping you want to change.

Sizing handles appear on the top, bottom, right, and left edges, and in each corner of the selected graphic. The sizing handles in the corners crop the graphic proportionally, while the sizing handles on the top, bottom, left, and right edges crop the graphic vertically and horizontally.

2. Hold **Shift** .... Shift
3. Move mouse on top of sizing handle until pointer changes to a ⌗
4. Hold left mouse button.
5. Drag to desired cropping.
6. Release mouse button.

The cropping dimensions display as percentages in the status bar.

RESET

Removes cropping and returns a graphic to its original size.

1. Click graphic you want to reset.
2. Hold **Ctrl** .... Ctrl
3. Double-click graphic.

INSERT DATABASE

Database information can be inserted into a Word document as a table from another Word document, database, spreadsheet, or other source of data.

Insert Database Command

1. Place cursor in document where you want to insert database.

2. Click **Insert Database** button .... in **Database** toolbar.

   OR

   a. Click **Insert** menu .... `Alt`+`I`

   b. Click **Database** .... `D`

   The Database dialog box displays.

3. Click `Get Data...` .... `Alt`+`G`

   The Open Data Source dialog box displays.

4. Follow procedures under **FILE OPEN**, page 35, to select desired database.

5. Click `OK` .... `↵`

   NOTES: Depending on the selected file type, you may also receive additional dialog boxes asking you to confirm the data source or prompting you for a password.

   If Word can't recognize field and record delimiters (characters that separate data) in text-delimited files, you are prompted to select the appropriate delimiters.

The Database dialog box redisplays.

continued...

244

6. Click ┃ **Table AutoFormat...** ┃ .... `Alt` + `T`
   if you want to apply an **AutoFormat** to
   the table that is inserted for the database. *(See TABLE*
   AUTOFORMAT, page 160, for more information.)

7. Click ┃ **Insert Data...** ┃ .... `Alt` + `I`

   *NOTE: The **Insert Data** dialog box displays.*

8. Click **A**ll .... `Alt` + `A`
   to insert all records in selected database file.

   OR

   a. Click **F**rom text box .... `Alt` + `F`
   b. Type starting record number .... *number*

   c. Click **T**o text box.................................... `Alt` + `T`
   d. Type ending record number .... *number*

9. Click **I**nsert Data as Field check box .... `Alt` + `I`
   to link selected database file to its source.

   *NOTE: Selecting the **Insert Data as Field** check*
   *box inserts a **DATABASE** field into the*
   *document. (See **FIELDS**, page 88, for*
   more information.)

10. Click ┃ **OK** ┃ .... `↵`

Query Options

Selects various query options when inserting a database with the Insert Database command.

FILTER RECORDS

Specifies conditions determining which data records to insert from a data source.

1. Follow steps 1 through 5 under **Insert Database Command**, above.

2. Click **Query Options...** .... `Alt`+`Q`

The Query Options dialog box displays.

3. Click **Filter Records** tab .... `Alt`+`F`

4. Click desired field.................................... `↑` `↓`
   from **Field** drop-down list box.

5. Click comparison factor .... `Tab` then `↑` `↓`
   from **Comparison** drop-down list box.

6. Type value...................................... `Tab` then `↑` `↓`
   in **Compare To** drop-down list box.

   To add more conditions:

   a. Click first drop-down list box........................... `Tab`
      on next line.

   b. Click desired condition................................. `↑` `↓`

   c. Repeat steps 4 through 6.

   To remove all selected Filter Records options:

   Click **Clear All** .... `Alt`+`C`

7. Select any additional options under **Sort Records** tab or **Select Fields** tab.

8. Follow steps 6 through 10 under **Insert Database Command**, page 243.

SORT RECORDS

Selects data fields by which to sort the selected data records from the data source.

1. Follow steps 1 through 5 under **Insert Database Command,** page 243.

2. Click **Sort Records** tab .... `Alt`+`O`

3. Click **Sort By** drop-down list box .... `Alt`+`S`

4. Click first record .... `↑` `↓`
   by which to sort.

5. Choose sort direction from the following options:

   • Ascending .... `Alt`+`A`

   • Descending .... `Alt`+`D`

6. Click **Then By** drop-down list box .... `Alt`+`T`

7. Click second record .... `↑` `↓`
   by which to sort.

8. Choose sort direction from the following options:

   • Ascending .... `Alt`+`E`

   • Descending .... `Alt`+`N`

9. Click **Then By** drop-down list box .... `Alt`+`B`

10. Click third record .... `↑` `↓`
    by which to sort.

11. Choose sort direction from the following options:

    • Ascending .... `Alt`+`I`

    • Descending .... `Alt`+`G`

continued...

247

To remove all selected Sort Records options:

Click [**Clear All**] .... `Alt`+`C`

12. Select any additional options under **Filter Records** tab or **Select Fields** tab.

13. Follow steps 6 through 10 under **Insert Database Command**, page 243.

SELECT FIELDS

Adds and removes data fields to include from the selected data records in the data source.

1. Follow steps 1 through 5 under **Insert Database Command**, page 243.

2. Click **Select Fields** tab .... `Alt`+`L`

   To add fields:

   a. Click **Fields in Data Source** list box .... `Alt`+`D`

   b. Click field .... `↑` `↓`
      you want to add.

   c. Click [**Select ▶▶**] .... `Alt`+`S`

   OR

   Click [**Select All ▶▶**] .... `Alt`+`E`
   to add all fields from data source.

   To remove fields:

   a. Click **Select Fields** list box .... `Alt`+`L`

   b. Click field .... `↑` `↓`
      you want to remove.

continued...

248

QUERY OPTIONS (CONTINUED)

c. Click [**◄◄ Remove**] .... `Alt`+`R`

   OR

   Click [**◄◄ Remove All**] .... `Alt`+`E`
   to remove all fields from **Selected Fields** list.

*NOTE: Select multiple fields by holding down **Shift**
          with above procedures. Select multiple, non-
          contiguous fields by holding down **Ctrl** and
          clicking with the mouse.*

3. Click **Include Field Names** check box .... `Alt`+`I`
   to use field names from header row of
   data source as column headings
   for database table.

   To remove all selected Select Field options:
   Click [**Clear All**] .... `Alt`+`C`

4. Select any additional options under **Filter Records** tab or
   Sort Records tab.

5. Follow steps 6 through 10 under **Insert Database
   Command**, page 243.

INSERT FILE

*Inserts files or sections of files into the current document. Files can be
other Word documents or from other applications.*

1. Click **Insert** menu .... `Alt`+`I`

2. Click **File** .... `L`

The Insert File dialog box displays.

3. Follow procedures under **OPEN FILE**, page 35.

4. Click **Link to File** check box .... `Alt`+`K`
   to link selected file to its source.

continued...

INSERT FILE (CONTINUED)

*NOTES: Selecting the **Link to File** check box inserts an **INCLUDE** field into the document. (See **FIELDS**, page 88, for more information.)*

5. Click **R**ange text box .... `Alt`+`R`
    to insert part of a file such as a bookmark from a Word file or a range from an Excel file.

6. Type appropriate identifier.

7. Click [**OK**] .... `↵`

INSERT PICTURE

Inserts pictures and graphics from other applications into the current document, as well as the various clipart files that come with Word.

1. Click **I**nsert menu .... `Alt`+`I`

2. Click **P**icture .... `P`

The Insert Picture dialog box displays.

3. Follow procedures under **OPEN FILE**, page 35.

4. Click **Lin**k to File check box .... `Alt`+`K`
    to link selected file to its source.

    *NOTES: Selecting the **Link to File** check box inserts an **INCLUDE** field into the document. (See **FIELDS**, page 88, for more information.)*

5. Click **Save with D**ocument .... `Alt`+`D`
    to store graphic in Word document along with link.

continued...

INSERT PICTURE (CONTINUED)

NOTES: The **Save with Document** option is only
available if **Link to File** check box has been
selected.

Selecting the **Save with Document** check
box increases the size of the Word file
since a complete representation of the
graphic is stored in the document.
Deselect this check box to decrease the
size of the Word file.

6. Click [OK] .... [↵]

PASTE SPECIAL

*Inserts information into a Word document with a variety of linking and
embedding options. Information can be from different sections of the
current document, or from other applications or Word files. (Also see
PASTE, page 16.)*

1. Select and copy desired information to Clipboard from
   source file or application. Ways of selecting information
   vary with different applications, but copying generally
   follows the same procedure in all Windows applications
   by selecting **Copy** from the **Edit** menu.

2. Place cursor in document where you want to paste
   selected information.

3. Click **Edit** menu... [Alt]+[E]

4. Click **Paste Special** .... [S]

The Paste Special dialog box displays.

5. Click **As** list box .... [Alt]+[A]

6. Click desired paste format .... [↑][↓]
   (available choices vary depending
   on information copied to the Clipboard)

continued...

251

NOTE: The **Result** section of the **Paste Special**
dialog box describes the results of each of
the available paste formats.

7.   Choose paste method from the following options:

- Paste .... `Alt`+`P`

- Paste Link .... `Alt`+`L`

NOTE: This option is only available if Clipboard
contents can be linked to data from an
external application.

8.   Click **Display as Icon** check box .... `Alt`+`D`
to display selected link as icon in document.

    To change icon representing link:

    a. Click `Change Icon...` .... `Alt`+`I`

    NOTE: This option is only available if **Display as
    Icon** check box has been selected.

The **Change Icon** dialog box displays.

    b. Click **Icon** list box .... `Alt`+`I`

    c. Click icon .... `↑` `↓`

The name of the file containing available icons appears at the bottom
of the dialog box.

    To search for other files containing icons:

    Click `Browse...` .... `Alt`+`B`

    d. Click **Caption** text box.......................... `Alt`+`C`
    to change caption for selected icon.

    e. Type caption .... text

continued...

PASTE SPECIAL (CONTINUED)

f. Click [**OK**] .... ⏎
to close **Change Icon** dialog box.

9. Click [**OK**] .... ⏎
to paste Clipboard contents with selected options.

SUPPLEMENTARY APPLICATIONS

*Word comes with three supplementary applications (or **applets**):*
WordArt 2.0, Equation Editor 2.0, and Graph 5.0. Applets can only
be run from within an application that supports OLE and cannot be
run as stand-alone applications. Information created with each of the
applets is inserted into a document as an embedded object. (See
EMBEDDED OBJECTS, page 233, for more information.)

> *NOTE: The following instructions are basic*
> *procedures for creating embedded objects*
> *with each of the applets.*

Equation Editor 2.0

*Creates an Equation Editor object. **Equation Editor** is used for*
building complex equations such as exponents, integrals, and other
mathematical elements.

1. Place cursor in document where you want to insert
equation.

2. Click **Insert** menu... Alt + I

3. Click **Object** .... O

4. Click **Create New** tab .... Alt + C

5. Click **Microsoft Equation 2.0**........................... ↑ ↓
from **Object Type** list box.

6. Click [**OK**] .... ⏎

The Equation Editor toolbar and menu bar displays.

continued...

EQUATION EDITOR 2.0 (CONTINUED)

7. Create equation by typing text and choosing desired templates, symbols, and operators from **Equation Editor** toolbar and menus. The **Equation Editor** toolbar buttons and their associated commands are as follows:

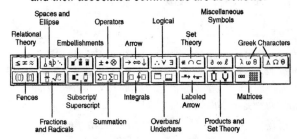

NOTES: *Clicking any of the above buttons displays a grid containing various choices for each of the categories.*

(See your Word documentation or on-line **Help** *for more information on using the* **Equation Editor** *toolbar along with the available commands in the* **Equation Editor** *menu.)*

8. After creating desired equation, click anywhere in the document window to exit **Equation Editor**.

Graph 5.0

Creates various types of charts (pie, line, bar, etc.) which can be created from an existing table in a Word document or from data imported from another application.

(See your Word documentation or on-line **Help** *for more information on using* **Graph**.*)*

1. Select a table containing data with which you want to create a chart, or place cursor in document where you want to insert a chart.

2. Click **I**nsert menu.. Alt + I

3. Click **O**bject... O

continued...

GRAPH 5.0 (CONTINUED)

4. Click **Create New** tab .... `Alt`+`C`

5. Click **Microsoft Graph 5.0** .... `↑``↓`
   from **Object Type** list box.

6. Click [**OK**] .... `←|`

The Graph window displays, containing a datasheet and chart window. If you selected a table in step 1, Graph creates a sample chart using the data contained in the table. If a table was not selected in step 1, Graph creates a sample chart using sample data.

> *NOTE: Data can also be imported from other applications using the File menu.*

7. Select desired chart type from **Gallery** menu.

8. Choose desired options from the various menus.

9. After creating desired chart, click anywhere in the document window to exit **Graph**.

WordArt 2.0

Creates stylized text effects in a document. Text can be formatted in a variety of different styles, shapes, alignments, and other effects.

1. Place cursor in document where you want to insert stylized text.

2. Click **Insert** menu .... `Alt`+`I`

3. Click **Object** .... `O`

4. Click **Create New** tab .... `Alt`+`C`

5. Click **Microsoft WordArt 2.0** .... `↑``↓`
   from **Object Type** list box.

6. Click [**OK**] .... `←|`

The Enter Your Text Here dialog box displays, along with the WordArt toolbar and menu bar

continued..

7. Type text .... *text*
   in text entry box.

   To insert special character:

   Click 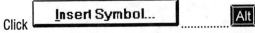 .... **Alt** + **I**

8. Choose desired text effect options from **WordArt** toolbar
   and menu. The **WordArt** toolbar buttons and their
   associated commands are as follows:

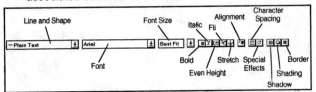

> *NOTE:* *Refer to your Word documentation or on-*
> *line **Help** for more information on using*
> *the **WordArt** toolbar along with the*
> *available commands in the **WordArt** menu.*

   **To update stylized text in Word document before
   exiting WordArt:**

   Click  .... **Alt** + **U**

9. After applying desired style effects, click anywhere in the
   document window to exit **WordArt**.

PROGRAM OPTIONS

AUTOFORMAT OPTIONS

Selects various rules for applying AutoFormats. (See AutoFormat, page 131, for more information).

AutoFormat

1. Click **Tools** menu .... `Alt`+`T`

2. Click **Options** .... `O`
   The Options dialog box displays.

3. Click **AutoFormat** tab .... `↑` `↓` `←` `→`

4. Click **AutoFormat** .... `Alt`+`A`

5. Choose from the following **Apply As You Type** options:

   - Hea**d**ings .... `Alt`+`D`

   - **L**ists .... `Alt`+`L`

   - Automatic **B**ulleted Lists .... `Alt`+`B`

   - Other **P**aragraphs .... `Alt`+`P`

6. Choose from the following **Replace As You Type** options:

   - Straight Quotes with 'Smart Quotes' .... `Alt`+`G`

   - **O**rdinals (1st) with Superscript .... `Alt`+`O`

   - **F**ractions (1/2) with .... `Alt`+`F`
     fraction character (½)

   - S**y**mbol Characters with Symbols .... `Alt`+`Y`

   To keep styles that have already been applied in a document:

   Click **S**tyles .... `Alt`+`S`

7. Click [**OK**] .... `↵`

AutoFormat As You Type

1. Click **Tools** menu .... `Alt` + `T`

2. Click **Options** .... `O`
   The Options dialog box displays.

3. Click **AutoFormat** tab .... `↑` `↓` `←` `→`

4. Click **AutoFormat As You Type** .... `Alt` + `T`

5. Choose from the following **Apply As You Type** options:

   - Headings .... `Alt` + `D`

   - Borders .... `Alt` + `R`

   - Automatic Bulleted Lists .... `Alt` + `B`

   - Automatic Numbered Lists .... `Alt` + `N`

6. Choose from the following **Replace As You Type** options:

   - Straight Quotes with 'Smart Quotes' .... `Alt` + `G`

   - Ordinals (1st) with Superscript .... `Alt` + `O`

   - Fractions (1/2) with .... `Alt` + `F`
     fraction character (½)

   - Symbol Characters with Symbols .... `Alt` + `Y`

7. Click [OK] .... `↵`

COMPATIBILITY

Determines how to display documents from earlier versions of Word and other word processing programs. Also determines font substitution for the active document if the document contains fonts that are not resident in your computer.

Display Compatibility

1. Click **Tools** menu .... `Alt`+`T`

2. Click **Options** .... `O`

The Options dialog box displays.

3. Click **Compatibility** tab .... `↑` `↓` `←` `→`

4. Click **Recommended Options For** .... `Alt`+`M`
   drop-down list box.

5. Click application .... `↑` `↓`

6. Click **Options** list box .... `Alt`+`O`

7. Choose desired options .... `↑` `↓`

   To use selected options as default settings for the current document and all new documents based on current template:

   a. Click **Default...** .... `Alt`+`D`

   b. Click **Yes** .... `Alt`+`Y`
      when confirmation dialog box appears.

8. Click **OK** .... `↵`

Font Substitution

1. Click **Tools** menu .... `Alt`+`T`

2. Click **Options** .... `O`

The Options dialog box displays.

continued...

FONT SUBSTITUTION (CONTINUED)

3. Click **Compatibility** tab .... ⬆️ ⬇️

4. Click [**Font Substitution...**] .... Alt + S

    NOTE: *The **Font Substitution** dialog box displays*
    if the document contains fonts requiring
    substitution. If no font substitution is
    necessary, you receive the following
    prompt:

    ┌────────────────────────────────────┐
    │ ▬   Microsoft Word   │
    ├────────────────────────────────────┤
    │ ⓘ No font substitution is necessary. All fonts used in this │
    │   document are available.   │
    │   │
    │   [OK]   [Help]   │
    └────────────────────────────────────┘

5. Click **Missing Document Font** list box .... Alt + M

6. Click font.. ⬆️ ⬇️
    for which you want to change font substitution.

7. Click **Subsituted Font** drop-down list box ..... Alt + S

8. Click substitute font .... ⬆️ ⬇️

9. Repeat steps 5 through 8 for other fonts for which you
    want to change font subsitution.

10. Click [**Convert Permanently...**] .... Alt + P
    if you want to replace missing document
    fonts with substituted fonts permanently.

11. Click [**OK**] .... ↵
    to close **Fonts Substitution** dialog box.

12. Click [**OK**] .... ↵
    to close **Options** dialog box.

CUSTOMIZE

Commands, styles, macros, and other information can be added and deleted from menus, assigned to shortcut keys, or added to toolbars.

> NOTE: The procedures in this manual cover the
> standard Word configuration.

Toolbars

1. Click **Tools** menu .... `Alt`+`T`

2. Click **Customize** .... `C`
    The Customize dialog box displays.

3. Click **Toolbars** tab .... `Alt`+`T`

4. Click **Categories** list box .... `Alt`+`C`

5. Click category .... `↑` `↓`

6. Drag button to desired toolbar.

    > NOTES: The toolbar to which you want to assign a
    > new button must be visible.
    >
    > Dragging a button to a blank area of the
    > screen creates a new toolbar.

7. Repeat steps 5 and 6 for additional categories and
    buttons.

    To remove toolbar buttons:

    a. Point at button you want to remove.

    b. Hold left mouse button.

    c. Drag button off toolbar to a blank area of screen and
        release mouse button.

8. Click **Save Changes In** drop-down list box... `Alt`+`V`

9. Click template .... `↑` `↓`
    where you want to save changes.

10. Click [Close] .... `↵`

Menus

1. Click **Tools** menu .... `Alt` + `T`

2. Click **Customize** .... `C`

The Customize dialog box displays.

3. Click **Menus** tab .... `Alt` + `M`

4. Click **Categories** list box .... `Alt` + `C`

5. Click category .... `↑` `↓`

6. Click **Commands** list box .... `Alt` + `O`

7. Click command .... `↑` `↓`

8. Click **Change What Menu** .... `Alt` + `U`
   drop-down list box.

9. Click menu to change.................................... `↑` `↓`

10. Click **Position on Menu** drop-down list box .. `Alt` + `P`

11. Click option .... `↑` `↓`

12. Click **Name on Menu** drop-down list box...... `Alt` + `N`

13. Type menu name .... *text*

   NOTE: *Place an ampersand (&) before the letter*
   you want underlined for the new menu
   item.

14. Click **Save Changes In** drop-down list box ... `Alt` + `V`

15. Click template.. `↑` `↓`
   where you want to save changes.

continued...

MENUS (CONTINUED)

16. Click [Add] .... Alt + A

    OR

    Click [Add Below] .... Alt + A

    **To add, delete, or rename menus
    on the main menu bar:**

    Click [Menu Bar...] .... Alt + B

    To rename a menu item:

    a. Follow steps 4 through 7.

    b. Click **Name on Menu** .... Alt + N
       drop-down list box

    c. Type new menu name .... *text*

    d. [Rename] .... Alt + A

    To remove a menu item:

    a. Follow steps 4 through 7.

    b. Click [Remove] .... Alt + R

    To reset all custom menu assignments:

    Click [Reset All...] .... Alt + S

17. Click [Close] .... ↵

Keyboard

1. Click **Tools** menu .... Alt + T

2. Click **Customize** C

   The Customize dialog box displays.

3. Click **Keyboard** tab .... Alt + K

4. Click **Categories** list box .... Alt + C

continued...

5. Click category .... ⬆️ ⬇️

6. Click **Commands** list box .... Alt + O

7. Click command .... ⬆️ ⬇️

8. Click **Press New Shortcut Key** .... Alt + N
   drop-down list box.

9. Press keystrokes you want to assign as shortcut keys.
   Currently assigned keystrokes are visible in **Current
   Keys** list box.

10. Click **Save Changes In** drop-down list box ... Alt + V

11. Click template.. ⬆️ ⬇️
    where you want to save changes.

12. Click [Assign] .... Alt + A

    To remove a shortcut key assignment:

    a. Follow steps 4 through 7.

    b. Click [Remove] .... Alt + R

    To reset all custom shortcut key assignments:

    Click [Reset All...] .... Alt + S

13. Click [Close] .... ⏎

264

EDIT OPTIONS

1. Click **Tools** menu .... `Alt`+`T`

2. Click **Options** .... `O`

The Options dialog box displays.

3. Click **Edit** tab.................................... `↑` `↓` `←` `→`

4. Choose from the following **Editing Options**:

   • **T**yping Replaces Selection .... `Alt`+`T`

   • **D**rag-and-Drop Text Editing .... `Alt`+`D`

   • Automatic **W**ord Selection...................... `Alt`+`W`

   • **U**se INS Key for Paste .... `Alt`+`U`

   • **O**vertype Mode.. `Alt`+`O`

   • Use **S**mart Cut and Paste .... `Alt`+`S`

   • Use Tab and Backspace Keys.................. `Alt`+`I`
     to Set Left **I**ndent

   • Allow **A**ccented Uppercase...................... `Alt`+`A`

5. Click **Picture Editor** drop-down list box .... `Alt`+`P`

6. Choose application you want to use as the picture editor.

   *NOTE: Choices vary depending on what
   applications you have installed.*

7. Click [**OK**] .... `↵`

FILE LOCATIONS

Modifies the default storage locations for various items you create or use in Word.

1. Click **T**ools menu .... `Alt` + `T`

2. Click **O**ptions.. `O`
The Options dialog box displays.

3. Click **File Locations** tab .... `↑` `↓` `←` `→`

4. Click **F**ile Types list box............................... `Alt` + `F`

5. Click file type whose default storage .... `↑` `↓`
   location you want to change.

6. Click [**Modify...**] .... `Alt` + `M`

*The **Modify Location** dialog box displays.*

7. Type drive and directory .... *drive* `:` `\` *directory*
   where you want to store the file type.

   OR

   a. Click **Dri**v**es** drop-down list box.............. `Alt` + `V`

   b. Type or Click drive letter .... *drive* or `↑` `↓`

   c. Double-click directory where you want to store file
      type in **Directories** list box.

   To create a new directory:

   a. Click [**New** ...] .... `Alt` + `N`

      *The **Create Directory** dialog box displays.*

   b. Type new directory name....................................*name*
      in **Name** text box.

   c. Click [**OK**] .... `↵`
      to close **Create Directory** dialog box.

8. Click [**OK**] .... `↵`
   to close **Options** dialog box.

GENERAL OPTIONS

1. Click **Tools** menu .... `Alt` + `T`

2. Click **Options** .... `O`

The Options dialog box displays.

3. Click **General** tab .... `↑` `↓` `←` `→`

4. Choose from the following **General** options:

- **Background Repagination** .... `Alt` + `B`

- Help for **WordPerfect** Users .... `Alt` + `W`

- Na**v**igation Keys for WordPerfect Users `Alt` + `V`

- Bl**u**e Background, White Text .... `Alt` + `U`

- Beep on Error **A**ctions .... `Alt` + `A`

- C**o**nfirm Conversions at Open .... `Alt` + `O`

- Update Automatic **L**inks at Open .... `Alt` + `L`

- Mail as A**t**tachment .... `Alt` + `T`

- **R**ecently Used File List .... `Alt` + `R`
  Type number .... *number*

- TipWi**z**ard Active .... `Alt` + `Z`

5. Click **Measurement Units** .... `Alt` + `M`
   drop-down list box.

6. Click desired measurement unit .... `↑` `↓`

7. Click [**OK**] .... `↵`

GRAMMAR OPTIONS

*(See **GRAMMAR**, page 191, for more information.)*

1. Click **T**ools menu .... `Alt` + `T`

2. Click **O**ptions .... `O`

The Options dialog box displays.

3. Click **Grammar** tab .... `↑` `↓` `←` `→`

4. Click **U**se Grammar and Style Rules .... `Alt` + `U`
   drop-down list box.

5. Click desired grammar and style rule .... `↑` `↓`

6. Choose from the following grammar and style rule
   options:

   • Check **S**pelling .... `Alt` + `S`

   • Show **R**eadability Statistics .... `Alt` + `R`

7. Click **Cus**tomize Settings... .... `Alt` + `T`
   to customize grammar and style rules.

The Customize Grammar Settings dialog box displays.

8. Choose grammar and style rule settings.

9. Click **OK** .... `↵`
   to close **Customize Grammar Settings** dialog box.

10. Click **OK** .... `↵`
    to close **Options** dialog box.

268

PRINT OPTIONS

*(See **PRINT**, page 17, for more information.)*

1. Click **T**ools menu .... `Alt`+`T`

2. Click **O**ptions .... `O`
   The Options dialog box displays.

3. Click **P**rint tab .... `↑` `↓` `←` `→`

4. Choose from the the following **Printing Options**:

   - **D**raft Print .... `Alt`+`D`

   - **R**everse Print Order .... `Alt`+`R`

   - **U**pdate Fields .... `Alt`+`U`

   - Update **L**inks... `Alt`+`L`

   - **B**ackground Printing .... `Alt`+`B`

5. Choose from the following **Include with Document** options:

   - **S**ummary Info...................................... `Alt`+`S`

   - **F**ield Codes .... `Alt`+`F`

   - **A**nnotations.. `Alt`+`A`

   - H**i**dden Text.. `Alt`+`I`

   - Drawing **O**bjects.................................... `Alt`+`O`

6. Click **Print Data Only for Forms**.................. `Alt`+`P`
   in **Options for Current Document Only**
   option box, if desired.

7. Click **Default Tray** drop-down list box .... `Alt`+`T`

8. Choose desired paper tray

   *NOTE: Choices vary depending on what type of
            printer you use.*

9. Click ` OK ` .... `↵`

REVISION OPTIONS

*(See **REVISIONS**, page 198, for more information.)*

> NOTE: For the following available color choices, selecting **By Author** assigns a unique color to the first eight people who revise a document. If more than eight people revise a document, the colors start over with the first color assigned.

1. Click **T**ools menu .... `Alt`+`T`

2. Click **O**ptions... `O`

*The **Options** dialog box displays.*

3. Click **Revisions** tab .... `↑` `↓` `←` `→`

4. Choose **Inserted Text** options:

   a. Click **M**ark drop-down list box.................. `Alt`+`M`

   b. Click desired format to mark new text......... `↑` `↓`

   c. Click **Co**lor drop-down list box .... `Alt`+`O`

   d. Click color.. `↑` `↓`
      to mark new text.

5. Choose **Deleted Text** options:

   a. Click **Ma**rk drop-down list box................. `Alt`+`A`

   b. Click desired format to mark deleted text.... `↑` `↓`

   c. Click **Co**lor drop-down list box .... `Alt`+`L`

   d. Click color.. `↑` `↓`
      to mark deleted text.

6. Choose **Revised Lines** options:

   a. Click **Mar**k drop-down list box................. `Alt`+`K`

continued...

REVISION OPTIONS (CONTINUED)

b. Click desired format .... ⬆️ ⬇️
   to mark lines containing revised text

c. Click **Color** drop-down list box .... Alt + R

d. Click color .... ⬆️ ⬇️
   to mark lines containing revised text.

7. Click **Highlight Color** .... Alt + I

8. Click color... ⬆️ ⬇️
   to highlight text.

9. Click [**OK**] .... ⏎

SAVE OPTIONS
(See MANAGE FILES, page 25, for more information.)

1. Click **Tools** menu .... Alt + T

2. Click **Options** .... O
   The Options dialog box displays.

3. Click **Save** tab .... ⬆️ ⬇️ ⬅️ ➡️

4. Choose from the following save options:

   • **Always Create Backup Copy**.................. Alt + B

   • **Allow Fast Saves**.................................. Alt + F

   • **Prompt for Document Properties** .... Alt + I

   • **Prompt to Save Normal Template** .... Alt + O

   • **Save Native Picture Formats Only**........ Alt + N

   • **Embed TrueType Fonts** .... Alt + E

   • **Save Data Only for Forms**..................... Alt + D

   • **Automatic Save Every** _____ .... Alt + S

     Type number in minutes............................. *number*
     for save interval (default is **10 minutes**).

continued...

271

5. Choose **File Sharing Options** for current document:

   a. Click **Protection Password** text box......... `Alt`+`P`
       to protect document from being
       opened by other users.

   b. Type password .... *password*

   c. Click **Write Reservation Password**.......... `Alt`+`W`
       text box to prevent unauthorized users
       from making changes to a document.

   d. Type password .... *password*

   NOTE: *Users who do not know the write
           reservation password can open a
           document by selecting the **Read Only**
           check box in the **File Open** dialog box.
           (See **OPEN FILE**, page 35, for more
           information.)*

   e. Click **Read-Only Recommended** .... `Alt`+`R`
       check box to recommend, but not require, that users
       open a document as read-only.

6. Click [**OK**] .... `↵`

SPELLING OPTIONS

*(See **SPELLING**, page 203, for more information.)*

1. Click **Tools** menu .... `Alt`+`T`

2. Click **Options**....................................... `O`

*The **Options** dialog box displays.*

3. Click **Spelling** tab............................... `↑` `↓` `←` `→`

continued...

272

SPELLING OPTIONS (CONTINUED)

4. Choose from the following **Automatic Spell Checking** options:

   - Automatic Spell Checking........................ `Alt`+`A`

   - Hide Spelling Errors in .... `Alt`+`S`
     Current Document

5. Choose from the following **Suggest** options:

   - Always Suggest. .... `Alt`+`L`

   - From Main Dictionary Only...................... `Alt`+`M`

6. Choose from the following **Ignore** options:

   - Words in UPPERCASE .... `Alt`+`U`

   - Words with Numbers .... `Alt`+`B`

   - **Reset Ignore All...** .... `Alt`+`I`
     to reset **Ignore All** list created during
     current Word session.

7. Choose from the following **Custom Dictionaries** options:

   To select custom dictionaries to use when spell checking:

8. Click **Custom Dictionaries...** .... `Alt`+`D`
   to select custom dictionaries to use when
   spell checking.

   The Custom Dictionaries dialog box displays.

9. Click desired dictionaries .... `↑` `↓` then `Space`

   To create new custom dictionary:

   a. Click **New...** .... `Alt`+`N`

continued...

SPELLING OPTIONS (CONTINUED)

*The **Create Custom Dictionary** dialog box displays.*

b. Click **Drives** drop-down list box............... `Alt`+`V`

c. Type or Click drive letter .... *drive* or `↑``↓`
   where you want to store the new dictionary.

d. Double-click directory in **Directories** list box where
   you want to store new dictionary.

e. Click **File Name** list box........................... `Alt`+`N`

f. Type name......................................*name*
   for new dictionary.

g. Click [**OK**] .... `↵`
   to close **Create Custom Dictionary** dialog box.

To edit custom dictionary:

a. Click **Custom Dictionaries** list box .... `Alt`+`D`

b. Click custom dictionary .... `↑``↓` then `Space`
   you want to edit.

c. Click [**Edit**] .... `Alt`+`E`

d. Make desired changes to custom dictionary.

e. Save and close the dictionary file.

To add custom dictionary:

a. Click [**Add...**] .... `Alt`+`A`

b. Click **Drives** drop-down list box............... `Alt`+`V`

c. Type or Click drive letter .... *drive* or `↑``↓`
   containing custom dictionary file
   you want to open.

d. Double-click directory in **Directories** list box
   containing custom dictionary file you want to open.

continued...

SPELLING OPTIONS (CONTINUED)

  e. Double-click desired custom dictionary file in **File Name** list box.

To remove custom dictionary:

  a. Click **Custom Dictionaries** list box .... `Alt`+`D`

  b. Click custom dictionary .... `↑` `↓`
     you want to remove.

  c. Click `Remove` .... `Alt`+`R`

To select language for custom dictionary:

  a. Click **Language** drop-down list box .... `Alt`+`G`

  b. Click desired language............................. `↑` `↓`

  NOTE: Language spell checking only applies to text that has been formatted in that language. (See LANGUAGE, page 195, for more information.)

10. Click `OK` .... `↵`
    to close **Custom Dictionaries** dialog box.

11. Click `OK` .... `↵`
    to close **Options** dialog box.

USER INFO

Changes information about the primary user.

1. Click **Tools** menu .... `Alt`+`T`

2. Click **Options** .... `O`

The Options dialog box displays.

3. Click **User Info** tab .... `↑` `↓` `←` `→`

continued...

4. Click **Name** text box.................................... `Alt` + `N`
   to choose the name Word uses as the
   author in the **Properties** dialog box when
   creating new documents. *(See PROPERTIES,
   page 39, for more information.)*

5. Type user name .... *user name*

6. Click **Initials** text box.................................... `Alt` + `I`
   to choose initials Word uses for
   annotation marks. *(See ANNOTATIONS,
   page 188, for more information.)*

7. Type user initials .... *user initials*

8. Click **Mailing Address** text box...................... `Alt` + `M`
   to choose the address Word uses
   when creating envelopes. *(See ENVELOPES AND
   LABELS, page 209, for more information.)*

9. Type mailing address ....*address*

10. Click [**OK**] .... `↵`

VIEW OPTIONS

(See DISPLAY OPTIONS, page 52, for more information.)

1. Click **Tools** menu .... `Alt` + `T`

2. Click **Options**.. `O`
   The Options dialog box displays.

3. Click **View** tab .... `↑` `↓` `←` `→`

continued...

VIEW OPTIONS (CONTINUED)

4 . Choose from the following **Show** options:

- **Draft Font** .... Alt + D

- **Wrap to Window** .... Alt + W

- **Highlight** .... Alt + L

- **Picture Placeholders** .... Alt + P

- **Field Codes** .... Alt + F

- **Bookmarks** .... Alt + K

- **Field Shading** .... Alt + E

  Click desired **Field Shading** option .... ↑ ↓
  (options are **Never**, **Always**, **When Selected**).

5. Choose desired Window options:

- **Status Bar** .... Alt + B

- **Horizontal Scroll Bar** .... Alt + Z

- **Vertical Scroll Bar** .... Alt + V

- **Style Area Width** .... Alt + Y

  Type number .... *number*
  for style area width.

NOTE: *After selecting desired **Style Area Width**, it
can be adjusted using the mouse.*

continued.

6. Choose one of the following **Nonprinting Characters** options:

- Tab Characters .... `Alt` + `T`

- Spaces .... `Alt` + `S`

- Paragraph Marks .... `Alt` + `M`

- Optional Hyphens .... `Alt` + `O`

- Hidden Text .... `Alt` + `I`

- All .... `Alt` + `A`

NOTE: *Nonprinting characters can also be displayed by clicking the **Show/Hide** button on the **Standard** toolbar. (See **NONPRINTING CHARACTERS**, page 53, for more information.)*

7. Click [**OK**] .... `↵`

278

INDEX

continued...

continued...

280

continued...

continued...

282

continued...

continued...

284

continued...

continued...

286

continued...

continued...

continued...

More Quick Reference Guides

---------- **ORDER FORM** ----------

DDC Publishing   275 Madison Ave. NY, NY 10016 $10 ea.

QTY.	CAT. NO.	DESCRIPTION

☐ Check enclosed. Add $2.50 for post. & handling & $1 post. for ea. add. guide.
NY State res. add local sales tax.

☐ Visa   ☐ Mastercard   *100% Refund Guarantee*

No._____Exp._____

Name_____

Firm _____

Address_____

City, State, Zip _____

Phone (800)528-3897   Fax (800)528-3862   11/6